October 13, 1996

For Roger Brown
Regards
Keith O. Hary

The Honorable Francis Thomas. Photo by Matthew Brady.
Library of Congress Collection.

ANSWERING THE CALL
The Organization and
Recruiting of the Potomac Home Brigade
Maryland Volunteers

Summer and Fall, 1861

Primarily from Original Sources

A Substantial Number
In the Author's Collection

by

Keith O. Gary
BA, History
Frostburg State University
M. Ed., University of Maryland

Member Phi Alpha Theta, Honorary History Society
Member The Maryland Historical Society
Member The Historical Society of Frederick County
Member The Civil War Trust

HERITAGE BOOKS, INC.

Front cover photo by Keith O. Gary

Published 1996 by

HERITAGE BOOKS, INC.
1540E Pointer Ridge Place
Bowie, Maryland 20716
1-800-398-7709

ISBN 0-7884-0521-7

A Complete Catalog Listing Hundreds of Titles
On History, Genealogy, and Americana
Available Free Upon Request

CONTENTS

DEDICATION

This book is dedicated to the memory of the late Ernest Berger of Frederick, Maryland, who for many years operated a book shop at 151 North Market Street in that city. After retiring, he had a small rare book and document business on Court Street.

He was a well known antiquarian and philatelist. In addition, Ernie was an accomplished amateur painter, thespian, and a jazz pianist of great repute. I purchased the letters and documents in this collection from Ernie in the 1960's and '70's. His great love of local and Maryland history, and especially his willingness to sell the documents one or two at a time, ensured that the collection remained intact and made this book possible. I am indebted to Ernie Berger, my good friend and mentor, whose memory has inspired me to produce this work.

FOREWORD

This book has been thirty-five years in the making. I can recall becoming very interested in history at the beginning of my high school years. I was fortunate to be able to attend Frostburg State College (now Frostburg University) as a history major, tuition free, by agreeing to teach in Maryland for five years upon graduation. This obligation was duly performed by teaching history in the Frederick County Public Schools.

While growing up in Frederick from about the age of eight years, I remember my father and mother becoming very good friends of Ernest Berger, owner of Berger's Book Mart which was at that time the only book store in town. There were numerous social occasions in the company of Ernie and his wife Ruth, at which I remember being enthralled by his recounting of local historical events. My interest in Maryland history, especially during the Civil War, can be traced to these times.

Because of my connection to Frostburg, Ernie gave me, I think for my birthday, one of the letters written by John Huntley. This was the beginning of my collection of Potomac Home Brigade documents which comprises the core of this book. I have no idea how or where he acquired the letters, but, so far as I can determine from my research, they are unique, as no others were discovered. Perhaps, one can hope, the publication of this book will uncover additional material in private hands.

I have owned the documents for about twenty-five years. It has been only in the past year that I have felt compelled to share them. My object in presenting this work to the public is two-fold; first, to contribute in some small way to the body of historical knowledge of the Civil War, and second, to pay tribute to one of the finest human beings I have ever known. It is therefore, with a fervent hope that this dual function will be satisfactorily accomplished, that ANSWERING THE CALL is humbly offered.

Greenbelt, Maryland
April 27, 1996

PART I
THE POTOMAC HOME BRIGADE

View of the Colonial Barracks

at Frederick, Maryland and the site of the Military Hospital

Massachusetts Commandery Military Order of the Loyal Legion and

The U.S. Military History Institure

The Potomac Home Brigade Volunteers was
established on Friday, July 19, 1861, under the authority of
an order from Secretary of War Simon Cameron, by
Francis Thomas of Frederick, Md. Thomas, a former
Governor of Maryland in the early 1840's, and then a
member of Congress, advertised in the newspapers and by
printed handbills for volunteers to come forward to form
into the four regiments he was authorized to raise.

The Battle of Bull Run on July 21, 1861, two days
after Cameron's authorization, had the effect of imparting a
strong impetus to the recruiting of the First Regiment. As
the reader will note from the location of the places the
letters in the Gary Collection were written, Western
Maryland was a stronghold of Union support. Baltimore,
known as a place where many were Pro-Confederate, also
became a major recruiting center for the Brigade.

The July 24, 1861 edition of the Baltimore American
and Commercial Advertiser published the notice referred to
above and is mentioned specifically in one of the letters
which follows:

*MARYLAND AND VIRGINIA HOME GUARDS.- From
the subjoined letter of Hon. Simon Cameron, Secretary of
War, to Hon. Francis Thomas, member of Congress from
the Allegany District, it will be perceived that an
opportunity is afforded to the loyal citizens of Western
Maryland, and of the counties of Loudon, Jefferson,
Berkley, Morgan, Hardy and Hampshire, in the State of
Virginia, to organize four regiments as a Home Brigade,
under lawful authority, for the protection of their persons*

6

and property from the merciless depredations to which both have been too long exposed.

They are,- the document says,- " to be sustained in the vicinity [where enlisted] whilst in service," and it would be discreditable to the good and true men of Western Maryland, if they failed to avail themselves of this opportunity to defend their own houses and firesides. The Brigade will be on the same footing as troops of the regular army, with like pay, rations, equipment, &c. Any one desiring detailed information on this subject, must seek it by letter addressed to ex-Gov. Thomas, at Frederick, Md., where an officer of the United States Army will be stationed to furnish the required information in the absence of ex-Gov. Thomas, and to muster into service and arm each company as it is offered.

War Department,   }
Washington, July 19, 1861}

Hon. Francis Thomas:

You are hereby authorized to provide for the organization of four regiments of the loyal citizens resident on both sides of the Potomac River from the Monocacy to the western boundary of Maryland, for the protection of the canal and of the property and persons of loyal citizens of the neighborhood, and to be stationed in the vicinity whilst in the service.

The men will be permitted to elect their own company officers, the field-officers to be appointed by the President. Arms will be for-

warded as soon as practicable.

Respectfully,

Your obedient servant,

Simon Cameron,

Sec' y of War.

Author's note; The original of this letter has the following endorsement of the President:

The Secretary of War has my approbation to sign this letter.

A. Lincoln

Baltimore was a city of divided loyalties. On July 25, 1861, the Baltimore REPUBLICAN , a decidedly Pro-Southern paper, printed this item:

[FROM OUR SECOND EDITION OF YESTERDAY.]

(Special Dispatch)

"HOME GUARDS"

Frederick, July 24.- Ex.Gov. Thomas, representative from this District, has received authority from the President and Secretary of War, to organize four Regiments from the people of this District and certain neighboring counties of Virginia, to form a Home Brigade, the Field officers to be appointed by the President, and the government to furnish the arms. A recruiting office has accordingly been opened in this city. The real object of this is to oppress those who sympathise (sic) with the South.

Representative Thomas wrote a letter to Secretary Cameron on July 20, 1861. In it he recommended the appointment of William P. Maulsby as Colonel of the First Regiment and Charles E. Trail as Lieutenant Colonel. Lewis P. Fiery was proposed as Major. This letter has President Lincoln's endorsement on it: "Unless there be some reason, not known to me, let the appointments, as above suggested by Gen. Thomas, be made.

A. Lincoln"

The First Regiment of the Potomac Home Brigade was recruited and quartered in the Frederick vicinity at Camp Worman. On August 29, 1861, William P. Maulsby of Frederick was officially appointed Colonel of the Regiment by President Lincoln. Seven companies were initially mustered to form the Regiment with the following officers on the staff:

> William P. Maulsby Sr., Colonel
> George R. Dennis, Lieutenant-Colonel
> John A. Steiner, Major
> George T. Castle, Adjutant
> Thomas M. Wolfe, Quartermaster
> Jerningham Boon, Surgeon
> Jacob Baer, Assistant Surgeon

Charles E. Trail and Lewis P. Fiery's names do not appear on the Muster Role and thus, presumably, either declined to serve or were unable.

The Company Commanders were: Company A, Captain R. Elsworth Cook; Company B, Captain William

Glessner; Company C, Captain William T. Faithful;
Company D, Captain Charles H. Baugher; Company G,
Captain John I. Yellott; Company I, Captain Walter
Saunders; and Company K, Captain Charles Brown. Later,
George T. Castle became Quartermaster and William P.
Maulsby , Jr. was named Adjutant. Shortly after the
original seven companies were enrolled, Company E, under
Captain William H. H. Yontz, Company F, under Captain
Samuel G. Prather, and Company H, commanded by
Captain William M. Cronise were mustered in.

The casualties suffered by the First Regiment during
the course of the War were as follows: Three
commissioned officers and forty-two enlisted men killed,
and one commissioned officer and eighty-five enlisted
soldiers died of disease, wounds, or accidents. A total of
one hundred thirty-one men died during the War.

The other three regiments of the Brigade were
recruited and mustered in much the same manner as the
First Regiment.

The Second Regiment was organized in
Cumberland, Maryland between August 27 and October
31, 1861. Companies A, B, C, E, G, H, I, and K were
recruited in Allegany County. Company F, Cavalry, was
recruited at Hancock, Maryland, while Company D came
from Piedmont, Virginia. This Regiment was assigned to
duty in Western Virginia as part of the Army of Western
Virginia under the command of General B. F. Kelly.
The Second Regiment Field and Staff consisted of:

Thomas Johns, Colonel
Robert Bruce, Lieutenant-Colonel

10

G. Ellis Porter, Major

Theodore Luman, First Lieutenant

Orlando D. Robbins, Adjutant

Kennedy H. Butler, Quarter Master

Samuel P. Smith, Surgeon

Patrick A. Healey, Assistant Surgeon

Henry H. Hartsock, Sergeant Major

Gideon G. Frethy, Commissary Sergeant

Thomas E. Dugan, Drum Major

The officers commanding the companies were as follows:

Company A : Captain, Alexander Shaw; First Lieutenant, John Douglas; Second Lieutenant, Andrew Spier.

Company B : Captain, J. D. Roberts; First Lieutenant, James A. Morrow; Second Lieutenant, A. S. Gallion.

Company C : Captain, John H. Huntley; First Lieutenant, John Weir; Second Lieutenant, Richard C. Sansom.

Company D : Captain, B. B. Shaw; First Lieutenant, Robert Powell, Second Lieutenant, Mark Powell.

Company E : Captain, James C. Lynn, First Lieutenant, Theodore Luman; Second Lieutenant, George Couter.

Company F : Captain Lewis Dyche, First Lieutenant; Norval McKinley; Second Lieutenant, George D. Somers.

Company G : Captain C. G. McClellan; First Lieutenant, Robert Cowan, Second Lieutenant, Lloyd Mahaney.

Company H : Captain, George H. Bragonier; First Lieutenant, S. T. Little; Second Lieutenant, George W. McColloh.

Company I : Captain, J. F. McCulloh, First Lieutenant, James M. Shober; Second Lieutenant, John F. Troxell.

Company K : Captain P. B. Petrie; First Lieutenant, Jason G. Sawyer; Second Lieutenant, Moses Bickford.

Engagements in which the 2nd Regiment participated were Springfield, VA, August 23, 1861; Blue House, VA, August 26, 1861; South Branch Bridge, MD, October 26, 1861; Springfield, VA, October 26, 1861; South Branch Wire Bridge, VA, October 26, 1861; Great Cacapon Bridge, VA, January 4, 1862; Vance's Ford, near Romney, VA, September 17, 1862; Charlestown, VA, October 18, 1863; Summit Point, VA, October 7, 1863; Charlestown, VA, October 18, 1863; Burlington, VA, November 16, 1863; Ridgeville, VA, January 4, 1864; Moorefield Junction, VA, January 8, 1864; Medley, VA, January 30, 1864; Lynchburg, VA, June 18, 1864; Salem, VA, June 21, 1864; South Branch Bridge, VA, July 4, 1864; Sir John's Run, VA, July 6, 1864; Snicker's Gap, VA, July 18, 1864; Martinsburg, VA, 1864; Back Creek, Bridge, VA, 1864; Hancock, MD, 1864; Green Spring Run, VA, 1864.

Casualties suffered by the Second Regiment consisted of one commissioned officer and nine enlisted men killed in battle, and eighty-four enlisted personnel died from wounds, disease, or accident, for a total of ninety-four.

12

The following report of Colonel Thomas Johns is found in the <u>History of Allegany County</u> by Thomas and Williams. It is a description of the Second Regiment's skirmish at the South Branch bridge of October 26, 1861.

Headquarters

2 Regt. P.H. Brigade

Camp Thomas, Oct. 27, 1861.

Brig. Gen. C. M. Thruston:

Sir: In compliance with verbal orders received after consultation between Gen. Kelly and yourself, the night of the 25th inst., I concentrated 700 of my regiment at Camp at North Branch Bridge, and on the following morning at 5:30 o'clock marched in the direction of Romney, passing through Frankfort, upon arriving at a point one and one-half miles from Springfield. The rear of my column was fired into by the enemy from the heights of the road, wounding two men, detaining the column. About one hour was occupied in clearing the woods of the enemy and dressing the wounded. We marched thence through Springfield, seeing frequent signs of the enemy's horsemen in retreat towards the bridge over South Branch of the Potomac. Upon arriving within a half mile of the bridge, my flankers and skirmishers on the left and front discovered the enemy on the opposite side of the river, when a brisk fire at once commenced. About this time the guns of General Kelly's column in vicinity of Romney were heard. After skirmishing with the enemy across the river about half an hour, I determined to force our way over the bridge. The enemy numbering (by the best information we could get) from four to six hundred, including cavalry,

13

having beforehand prepared to defend its passage, had arranged covers for his riflemen on an eminence immediately fronting the bridge.

Captain Alexander Shaw, of Company A, who led the advance of the column to this point, was with his company, directed to lead the way across the bridge, at a double quick step. Supported by the remainder of the regiment, Captain Shaw promptly moved his company as directed, and when about half way across the bridge, discovered that a portion of the plank flooring on the further side had been removed. The enemy on discovering the movement, opened fire by volley, killing one and wounding six of my men, causing the company to seek shelter behind the parapets of the bridge.

After skirmishing some time from the parapets of the bridge and an eminence on our left, and not hearing the fire of Gen. Kelly for the previous hour, I concluded he had carried Romney, and the object of my march, to create a diversion in his favor being accomplished, I determined to retire, which I did, in good order, to Old Town in Maryland, arriving there about 9 o'clock P. M., after a march of 25 miles.

It is with pleasure that I speak of the good behavior of all my officers and men, and would call your attention particularly to the gallant charge led by Captain Alexander Shaw, Captain Fiery, of Dragoons, with his company, rendered very effective service by drawing the fire of the enemy from my regiment at the bridge. I was much gratified and indebted to Mr. Grehan, who volunteered to go with me, for his prompt and cheerful

assistance. Mr Grehan was frequently exposed to severe
fire of the enemy.

> *I am with great respect,*
>> *Your obedient servant,*
>>> *Thomas Johns,*

Colonel Second Regiment Potomac Home Brigade

This letter is reprinted with the permission of the Regional Publishing Company, Baltimore, Maryland.

The Third Regiment was organized at Cumberland, Hagerstown, and Baltimore between October 31, 1861, and May 20, 1862, with the exception of Companies I and K. I Company was recruited at Ellicott's Mills and K Company at Monrovia. Companies A, B, C, D, and H were enrolled from Allegany County, Company E from Hagerstown, Company G from Frederick County, and Company F from Baltimore.

Third Regiment Field and Staff Officers were the following:

Stephen W. Downey, Colonel

Charles Gilpin, Lt. Colonel

Charles L. Grafflin, Major

Nathaniel M. Ambrose, First Lieutenant and Adjutant

Benjamin F. Cook, Regimental Quarter Master

Carles E. S. McKee, Surgeon

Henry C. Stewart, Assistant Surgeon

George W. Anders, Sergeant Major

Julius T. C. Willman, Commissary Sergeant

Gustavus Valois, Quarter Master Sergeant

Franklin Jeffers, Hospital Steward

The Company Commanders of this Regiment were:

Company A : Captain, James S. Innskeep; First Lieutenant, John Coles; Second Lieutenant, William A. Cross.

Company B : Captain, William F. Cardiff; First Lieutenant, Moses Whitford, Second Lieutenant, John K. Whitford.

Company C : Captain, Harry C. Rizer; First Lieutenant, William R. Jarboe; Second Lieutenant, Charles F. McAleer.

Company D : Captain, Michael Fallon; First Lieutenant, Joseph L. Forsyth; Second Lieutenant, John M. Armstrong.

Company E : Captain, Henry B. McCoy; First Lieutenant, John W. Dodson; Second Lieutenant, Theodore Goff.

Company F : Captain, Robert Maxwell; First Lieutenant, Peter J. Mayberry; Second Lieutenant, William H. Foreman.

Company G : Captain, Jacob Sarbaugh; First Lieutenant, William H. Hipsley; Second Lieutenant, Joseph K. Pitman.

Company H : Captain, William A. Falkenstine; First Lieutenant, Frederick Pringey; Second Lieutenant, Hanson B. Friend.

The Third Regiment saw action in the following engagements: Franklin, VA, May 12, 1862; Wardensville,

VA, May 29, 1862; Moorefield, VA, June 29, 1862; Harper's Ferry, VA, September 13, 14, and 15, 1862; Frederick, MD, July 7 and 8, 1864; Battle of Monocacy, July 9, 1864; Snicker's Gap, July 18, 1864; Bolivar Heights, August 6, 1864; Halltown, VA, August 8, 1864, Charlestown, VA, August 9, 1864; and Berryville, VA, August 13, 1864.

The Third Regiment suffered one commissioned officer and eight enlisted men killed in battle, and one commissioned officer and seventy- three enlisted died of wounds, disease, or accidents. The total casualties for the War were eighty-three.

A Fourth Regiment was partially recruited with only three companies completed. Company A was enrolled in Hagerstown, Company B in Baltimore and Company C in Frederick County. This effort took place during the winter of 1861-62. While further attempts at recruitment were underway, the three Companies were assigned to guard duty along the Baltimore and Ohio Railroad between Harpers Ferry and Martinsburg, Virginia. On August 11, 1862 these three Companies were absorbed into the Third Regiment and the Fourth Regiment ceased to exist.

The Potomac Home Brigade was given the task of providing "for the protection of the Canal and of the property of loyal citizens of the neighborhood." It was assigned to act as a protective force to guard the Potomac and the C. & O. Canal from Confederate raids or inroads. This service was performed throughout the War at intervals, by the Brigade between the mouth of the

Monocacy River and Hancock, Maryland, the most likely route of invasion.

The First Regiment was attached to General Nathaniel Banks' Division as part of the regular U. S. Army. The official mustering in took place in Frederick on November 28, 1861, with Major Richard S. Smith acting as the Mustering Officer. 877 men were included in this muster. The Field and Staff Officers were as follows:

Colonel : William P. Maulsby,Sr.

Lieutenant-Colonel : George R. Dennis

Major : John A. Steiner

Adjutant : William P. Maulsby, Jr.

Quartermaster : Daniel Blocher

Surgeon : Jerningham Boon

Chaplain : William G. Ferguson

Assistant Surgeon : James Willard

Sergeant Major : Frank S. Blays

Quartermaster Sergeant : Robert Barnes, Jr.

Commissary Sergeant : Ira Tyler

Drum Major : Robert Shaeffer

General Banks was one of the Political Generals appointed by President Lincoln. He had his headquarters in Frederick during the latter part of 1861 and the early part of 1862. One of the most notable incidents during Banks' sojourn in Frederick was reported by the Baltimore American and Commercial Advertiser in the edition of September 19, 1861. The item reads:

A Military Movement and Arrests

A few minutes after the formality of opening the Legislature had been gone through with by the clerks, and

18

they dispersed, small squads of the Wisconsin Regiment,
each under charge of an officer, were observed moving
through the city, all taking different directions towards the
outskirts. Thus in about a half hour a cordon of armed
pickets circled the entire town, with instructions to allow
no one to pass out without a written permit from a member
of General Banks' staff, who had been appointed Provost
Marshall. This had scarcely been accomplished before a
squad of police officers from Baltimore consisting of
Lieutenant Carmichael, Sergeant Wallis, Sergeant Watt
and Officer West, accompanied by a military escort of the
Third Wisconsin Regiment, Colonel T. H. Ruger, which
has been encamped for some days near the rail road
depot, commenced to search the city for parties they were
ordered to arrest. In the course of the afternoon and
evening, and yesterday morning, the following arrests
were made.

> *Milton Y. Kidd, Clerk of the House*
> *William Kilgour, Clerk of the Senate*
> *John N. Brewer, Reading Clerk of the Senate*
> *S. P. Carmack, Assistant Clerk of the Senate*
> *William E. Salmon, of Fred'k., House of Delegates*
> *Thomas J. Claggett, "   "   "   "*
> *Andrew Kessler,   "   "   "   "*
> *Josiah H. Gordon, of Allegany,   "   "*
> *Richard C. MacCubbin, Anne Arundel, "*
> *D. Bernard Mills, of Carroll County,   "*
> *William R. Miller, of Cecil County,   "*
> *Clark J. Durant, St. Mary's County,   "*
> *J. Lawrence Jones, Talbot County,   "*

19

The following citizens were also arrested: John W. Elkins and John Hagan who had been very noisy, making threats &c, with E. A. Hanson, William Mason, William Hanson and his two sons.

E. Riley, editor of the Annapolis Republican and printer of the House, was also arrested.

The prisoners were all taken to the Barracks, as fast as arrested, and when Dr. Jones, of Talbot, was arrested on Wednesday morning about noon- he being the last except Mr. Mitchell, the Sergeant at Arms of the House, who could not be found, and is believed to have escaped- the guards around the town were withdrawn, and the ancient city of Frederick again fell back into the control of the civil authorities.

General Banks was given the authority to arrest disloyal members of the Legislature, then in session in Frederick, by Secretary of War Cameron. The relevant portion of this order reads: "The passage of any act of secession by the Legislature of Maryland must be prevented. If necessary, all or any part of the members must be arrested. Exercise your own judgment as to the time and manner, but do the work efficiently."

The arrests occurred on September 17, and Banks' report to the Secretary stated that "All members of the Maryland Legislature assembled at Frederick City on the 17th instant known or suspected to be disloyal in their relations to the Government have been arrested."

Elements of the First Regiment fought at Loudon Heights, Harpers Ferry, Winchester, Gettysburg, and

Monocacy. Captain Faithful of Company C was cited for his initiative and resourcefulness in removing horses and valuable stores from Frederick just before the city was occupied by Confederate troops under the command of Colonel Bradley T. Johnson in September, 1862. Johnson, a native of Frederick, had been a prominent attorney in the City before the War. His father was a brother of Thomas Johnson, first Governor of the State of Maryland. General Banks used Johnson's home at the corner of West Second and Court Streets as his headquarters and residence.

PART II
THE LETTERS

The following is a collection of letters largely from Western Maryland, some from Baltimore, and a few from Virginia, related to the call for recruitment of volunteer companies for the Brigade. Most are addressed to Francis Thomas, but several are addressed to his Mustering Officer, Major Richard S. Smith. Many of the letters are requests for further information about the procedures for mustering companies, others are offers to raise recruits, and still others are requests for appointment as officers. One letter from a Baltimore merchant is a dunning request for payment for flags addressed to Captain John I. Yellott, First Regiment, Company G.

The letters speak for themselves. They have never been published before. They are presented here in facsimile and as verbatim transcriptions to allow the reader to see them as originally written. The letters provide insight into the motives, whether patriotic, mercenary, or ambitious, of ordinary citizens experiencing probably the most momentous time in their lives. Reading them gives one a unique perspective not available in the better known "global" histories of the Civil War, and , it is hoped, will allow one to appreciate that persons leading simple, everyday lives can have an impact on history in a way they never would have imagined at the time.

Baltimore July 25th 1861

Hon Francis Thomas
        Frederick Md
                Sir

                    Will companies, recruited
in this city be acceptable in the "Home Brigade" which
you have been authorized to organize by the your
department,, and will the President commission the
officers.?

    Can any men be recruited here without interfering
with privileges granted Genl Cooper? Should the
services of any companies from here, be accepted;
will they have to proceed to Frederick to be Mustered
in; at their own expense, or will the Government
incur the liability.? Will the members of the Brigade
be placed on the same footing as the regular Army in
regard to pay, rations &c.?

    The undersigned has no doubt that any men raised
in this city for the Brigade, would be far superior
in mental and moral qualifications, to those
who are enlisting in the regular Md Volunteers.

    A Company of respectable young men, to act as Rifle-
-men could I think be organized at once

        Your prompt reply to the above will oblige
                    Yours Respectfully
                        William Craig

Box 1243 Balto Post Office

Baltimore July 25th 1861

Hon Francis Thomas

      Frederick, Md
          Sir
              Will companies recruited in this city be acceptable in the "Home Brigade" which you have been authorized to organize by the war department, and will the President comission the officers?

              Can any men be recruited here without interfering with priveleges granted Genl Cooper? Should the services of any companies from here be accepted, will they have to proceed to Frederick to be mustered in at their own expenses or will the government incur the liability? Will the members or the Brigade be placed on the same footing as the regular army in regard to pay, rations, etc?

              The undersigned has no doubt that any men raised in this city for the Brigade, would be far superior in mental and moral qualifications to those who are enlisting in the regular Md volunteers.

              A company of respectable young men to act as Riflemen could I think be organized at once.

              Your prompt reply to the above will oblige.

                        Yours Respectfully
                        William Craig

Box 1234 Balto Post Office

Baltimore July 21th /61

Hon Fr Thomas
Frederick city Md
                Sir
                    I hold a commission
as 1st Lieutenant duly signd by
by Governor T. G. Pratt and in that cap=
acity would offer myself to you in
forming a part of one of the
Regiments you are authorised to
raise as a Home Guard. I am a
native of Washington Co Md where
I received My commission My age
is 49 years, if you think I can
render you and My county service
I should be glad to received in
detail the requisite information

                    Respectfully
                    Saml L King
                    Balto Md

Baltimore   July 26th 1861

Hon F. Thomas
Frederick, Md
      Sir

        I hold a commission as the 1st Lieutenant duly signed by Governor T. G. Pratt and in that capacity would offer myself to you in forming a part of one of the Regiments you are authorized to raise as a home guard. I am a native of Washington Co. Md. where I received my commission. My age is 49 years, if you think I can render you and my country service, I should be glad to received in detail the requisite information.

                Respectfully
                Saml L. King

                Balto Md

Baltimore July 29/61

Hon. Francis Thomas.

Dear Sir.

As I perceive you are
endeavoring to raise certain
regiments for the U.S. service in
Western Md and elsewhere. I
venture to offer you my assistance
so far as it may be available.
I first thought of it through receiving
letters on the subject from Alleghany
where I first saw you— one in
particular from Mr. John Douglas
headminer at Lonaconing— highly
influential among the numerous miners
in the valley, and who has four sons has
already raised seventy men—
stating that my name would be of
much service in Alleghany Co.

I think I might promise to
raise a regiment in about a
month were I appointed Colonel
as these letters expressly stipulate
as many of the men place entire
confidence in me

Mr. Thos. Alexander
my uncle whom you know very
well advise me to write and
ask your recommendation to
secy Cameron for that purpose
I think yours alone amply
sufficient but if you think otherwise
I can easily obtain others.

My objects in this proposal
are first an honest desire to
serve my country and ~~and~~ besides
to assist the noble undertaking
you have begun. I wish other
members of Cong would do the
same. Yours very truly

F. W. Alexander

address
F. W. Alexander
Baltimore
md.

Baltimore July 29,1861

Hon Francis Thomas

Dear Sir

As I perceive you are endeavoring to raise certain regiments for the U. S. Service in Western Md. and elsewhere. I venture to offer you my assistance so far as it may be available. I first thought of it through receiving letters on the subject from Alleghany where I first saw you- one in particular from Mr. John Douglas head miner at Lonaconing- highly influential among the numerous miners in the valley and where Son has already raised seventy men- stating that my name would be of much service in Alleghany Co. I think I might promise to raise a regiment in about a month were I appointed Colonel as these letters expressly stipulate as many of the men place entire confidence in me.

Mr Thos. Alexander my uncle whom you know very well advises me to write and ask your recommendation to Sec'y Cameron for that purpose. I think yours alone amply sufficient, but if you think otherwise I can easily obtain others.

My objects in this proposal are first an honest desire to serve my country and besides to assist the noble undertaking you have begun. I wish others members of Cong. would do the same.

Yours very truly

F. W. Alexander

Baltimore, July 30th 1861

Hon. Francis Thomas
                    Sir
                        I would take it as
a great favour if you would be kind enough
to give me some information in reference to
the home Guards of this State whether those
of this City are to be included in your
bill or not as we have here already more than
a thousand but have no way to get any arms
even if they receive any pay. And if our home
guards are not included in your Regiments will
you receive any from this City. My Reason for
asking you these questions are that I am at present
acting as first Lieutenant of the home Guards of
the 11th Ward and the members wish to know whether
their organizing will amount to anything and what
steps they must take to get paid, armed
and equipped. please answer at your earliest convenience
                        Respectfully Yours
                        Wm. A. Hogarth
                        248 William Street Balt.

Baltimore July 30th 1861

Honor Francis Thomas
                    Sir
                              I would take it as a great favor if
you would be kind enough to give me some information in
refference to the home Guard of this state whether those of
this City are to be included in your bill or not as we have
here already more than a thousand but have know way to
get any arms and if they receive any pay or not if our home
guard are not included in your Regiment will you receive
any from this City My reason for asking you these
question are that I am at present acting As first Lieutenant
of the home guard of the 18th ward and the members wish
to know whether their organising will amount to anything
or what steps they must take to get properly armed and
equiped. Please answer at your earliest convenience.
                              Respectfully Yours
                              Wm. A. Hogarth
                              248 Hollins Street Balt.

To Brigadier General The Honorable
        D. Thomas.

Sir

        as the undersigned am commissioned
by the officers and men of my company
to address to you this letter offering to
your command our service.

        We are now organizing
a Rifle company of rifle, the officers and
almost all the men have seen active
service in regular European Army's

        Sir. if you accept the company
please let me know where to report
and by what means I am to transport
the men.

        I am most respectfull
                your obidient
                    [signature]
south-west corner of Gamen [illegible]
                Baltimore

33

To Brigadier General the Honorable

Mr. Thomas

Sir

I the undersigned am commissioned by the officers
and men of my company to address to you this letter
offering to your command our service.

We are now organizing a Rifle company of the
officers and almost all the man have seen active service in
regular European Army's.

Sir: if you accept the company please let me know
where to report and by with means I am to transport the
man.

I am most respectful
your obedien
J. Sudsburg

south-west corner of Gorman & Sharp
Baltimore

Westminster July 25

Hon Francis Thomas

Sir, Seeing the
Proclimation for home Guards
in the papers. I write to you for
the purpos of Knowing wether men
form Carroll County will be
acceptable or not. I am Capt of
the home Guard heare and there
are a great many men heare wants
me to form a company and go
I am my self a citizen of Frederick
and would like to go home for
that purpos, answer me as soon
as Convenient

Yours most Respectfully
James F. Lowell

Westminster July 25(1861)

Hon Francis Thomas

     Sir. Seeing the Proclamation for home Guards in
the paper, I write to you for the purpose of knowing
wether men from Carroll County will be acceptable or not.
I am Capt. of the home guard here and there are a great
many men here wants me to form a company and go. I am
myself a citizen of Frederick and would like to go home
for that purpose. Answer me as soon as convenient.

     Yours most Respectfully

     James P. Lowell

Uleverton Fred'k County
July 25th 1861

Hon'ble Francis A. Shinne

D' Sir

We are about forming a Company in this vicinity to volunteer as the "Home Brigade" which I see has been ordered by Sec'y Cameron, to guard the Canel & other property. The Rebel army have committed so many depredations in this neighborhood that all of our loyal Citizens wish to avail themselves of the present opportunity to put down all such lawless Acts

I have been requested to get all the detailed information on the subject from you. as to the duties required, the number of men required to make a Company, When in all probability we would be

required to Muster Pay &c and all
information necessary on the subject
Please let me hear from you as
early as Convenient as the People
here are anxious to form a Company
and have appointed me to get
what information I could Concern-
ning it.
I am very Respectfully
Yours
Alfred T. Spencer

38

Weverton Fredk. County Md.
July 25th 1861

Hon Francis Thomas

D'Sir

We are about forming a company in this vicinity to volunteer as the "Home Brigade". Which I see has been ordered by Sec'y. Cameron to guard the Canal and other property. The Rebel Army have committed so many depredations in this neighborhood that all of our loyal citizens wish to avail themselves of the present opportunity to put down all such lawless acts.

I have been requested to get all the detailed information on the subject from you as to the duties required, the number of men required to make a company. When in all probability we would be required to muster, pay etc. and all information necessary on the subject. Please let me hear from you as early as convenient as the people here are anxious to form a company and have appointed me to get what information I could concerning it.

I am Very Respectfully
Yours
Alfred F. Spencer

Petersville Frederick Co Md July 28/61

Sir

Having seen by the papers that
you are about to get up four regiments
as a home guard for the protection of
our State, I therefore offer myself as
quarter master, you having known
me for a long time. I think it unnecessary to say more just now, if I knew
when I could see you in Frederick I
would be there, but I will be in Washington
in about two weeks

Very respectfully yours

S. Thomas   Thos. Winter

40

Petersville Frederick Co. Md. July 26th '61

Sir

Having seen by the papers that you are about to get up your regiment as a home guard for the protection of our state, I therefore offer myself as quarter master. You having known me for a long time, I think it unnecessary to say more just now. If I knew when I could see you in Frederick, I would be there, but I will be in Washington in about two weeks.

Very Respectfully yours
Thos. Winter

F. Thomas

Creagerstown Frederick County
Md

Hon. Francis Thomas
dr Sir

Having noticed that you are to
provide a "Home Guard" for the
protection of persons & property
of the "Border", and believing that
a large number of men can be raised
in this portion of Fred'k Co, I write
to you for information upon the
subject, I feel It my duty as a
loyal Citizen to do Something towards
the Sustenance of our Government
but the responsibilities resting
upon me at home at this particular
time will not permit me to go abroad
to perform duty for my County, but
would desire from you an appointment
of some kind in this section of
Maryland for the good of the Cause
& the furtherance of the cause of the
Va & Md "Home Guards"
I am engaged in the Merchandising
business in this place & am also

Post Master here. Tho' should the
Office of P. M. interfere with an
appointment from you, I will
resign the office of P. M. immediately
Hoping to hear from you soon I
subscribe myself your Most obedient
To the   J. H. B. Otto
Honorable Francis Thoms

Creagerstown
Frederick County
Md.

Hon Francis Thomas

Dr Sir

Having noticed that you are to provide a "Home Guard"
for the protection of persons & property of the "Boarder",
and believing that a large number of men can be raised in
this portion of Fredk. Co. I write to you for information
upon the subject. I feel it my duty as a loyal citizen to do
something towards the sustenance of our Government but
the responsibilities resting upon me a home at this
particular time will not permit me to go abroad to purform
duty for my county, but would desire from you an
appointment of some kind in this section of Maryland for
the good of the country and the furtherance of the cause of
the Va. & Md. "Home Guards".

I am engaged in the merchandizing business in this place &
am also Post Master here tho should the office of P. M.
interfere with an appointment from you, I will resign the
office of P. Mr. immediately. Hoping to here from you
soon, I subscribe myself Your Most Obedient

J. H. B. Otto

To the
Honorable Francis

Thomas

27th July 1861

Clearspring Md

To Hon Frank Thomas

Sir

I notice in the
Baltimore American & Commercial
Advertiser a call for 4
Regiments of Volunteers on
the line of Virginia and
Maryland to Protect the Canal
& our Firesides &c.

I Simply ask if a company
of Cavalry is Required and at
on what Conditions

Yours with Respect
John D Ellis
Clearspring
Md

27th July, 1861
Clearspring, Md

To Hon. Frank Thomas

    Sir;

      I notice in the Baltimore American & Community Advertiser a call for a Regiment of volunteers on the line of Virginia and Maryland to protect the canal & our firesides etc.

      I simply ask if a company of Cavalry is required and on what conditions.

      Yours with Respect
        John D. Ellis
        Clearspring
        Md

Clearspring Md July 26 1861

Doctor F. Thomas

Sir

I am induced from the notice to loyal citizens of the western part of Maryland to form four regiments for the protection of the Canal and our own property to engage in the recruiting capacity if the emol-uments of the Office will justify to give up my business. My being raised in Virginia will enable me to be serviceable to you. If you stand in need of such assistance and can confer the favour upon me I will satisfy you by giving you good and substantial reference to my position in society and capabilities for filling such station

Yours truly

J. Rufus Smith

P.S. Please answer immediately

Clearspring, Md   July 26, 1861

Ex Gov F. Thomas
        D'Sir

            I am induced from the notice to loyal citizens
of the western part of Maryland to form four regiments for
the protection of the canal and over our own property to
engage in the recruiting capacity if the emoluments of the
office will justify to give up my business. My being raised
in Virginia will enable me to be of service to you. If you
stand in need of such assistance and can confer the favour
upon me I will satisfy you by giving you good and
substantial references to my position in society and
capabilities for filling such stations.

                              Yours Truly   J. Rufus Smith

P. S. Please answer immediately

Clear Spring Aug 5th /61

Hon. Francis Thomas.

Dr Sir

I have
been trying to raise a Volunteer
Company to be attached to one
of the Regiments of the Home
Brigade, and so far have
succeeded in getting about
forty names, and I now
write you asking for information
as to whether we must have
the full number 83 before
we can organize ourselves
into a company and be accepted
or could we not be organized
and be equipped and at
once commence drilling
and recruiting, I feel very

49

confident that I could soon
fill out the Company, at
least a great deal more
rapidly than under the
present circumstances,
the great difficulty that we
labour under is this, that
we cannot tell them with any
certainty when we shall get
into service or whether at
all or not, if we are compelled
to have the number that
comprises a Company to be
accepted. owing to this uncertainty
we have failed to procure
the names of a number of young
men who were out of employment,
and who have now enlisted
in the Companies forming at
Williamsport for Col. Vances

Regiment, several parts of those Companies have been equipped and have been through our place recruiting and filling up their Companies, having a decided advantage over us, as they can offer a certainty and pay to a recruit at once if he will enlist with them, and then too they excite more interest by being organized and equipped, and then their recruits are sworn in at once and have no time to deliberate and get out of the notion.

You will please give me some information upon the subject also any instructions that you may think proper to give will be faithfully carried out as I am determined

to use every effort in my
power to have our town and
district represented by
one Company, and located in the
Home Brigade.

I would just state here
that Doct. S. Jones handed
me your letter to him upon
the subject as soon as he
received it, and requested me
to try what I could do in
the way of raising a Company.

Hoping to hear from you
as early as convenient.

I remain your Obd Servt

S. G. Prather

To the
Hon. Francis Thomas

Clearspring Aug 5th/ 61

Hon Francis Thomas

Dr Sir

I have been trying to raise a
Volunteer Company to be attached to one of the
Regiments of the Home Brigade, and so far have
succeeded in getting about forty names, and I now write to
you asking for information as to whether we must have the
full number 83 before we can organize ourselves into a
company and be accepted or could we not be organized
and be equipped and at once commence drilling and
recruiting. I feel very confident that I could soon fill out
the company, at least a great deal more rapidly than under
the present circumstances. The great difficulty that we
labour under is this; that we cannot tell them under any
certainty when we shall get into service or whether at all or
not, if we are compelled to have the number that comprises
a company to be accepted. Owing to this uncertainty, we
have failed to procure the names of a number of young men
who were out of employment and who have now enlisted
in the Companies forming at Williamsport for Col. Lamon's
Regiment. Several parts of these companies have been
equipped and have been through our place recruiting and
filling up their companies, having a decided advantage over
us as they can offer a certainty and pay to a recruit at once
if he will enlist with them, and there too they excite more
interest by being organized and equipped, and then their

53

recruits are sworn in at once and have no time to deliberate and get out of the notion.

You will please give me some information on the subject also any instructions that you may think proper to give will be faithfully carried out as I am determined to use every effort in my power to have our Town and district represented by one Company at least in the Home Brigade.

I would just state here that Doct. J. Jones handed me your letter to him upon the subject as soon as he received it and requested me to try what I could do in the way of raising a Company. Hoping to hear from you as early as convenient

I remain your ob't serv't

S. G. Prather

Hagerstown Augt 10 1861

Dr Sir

I am requested to write
you on behalf of the residents of
this place to be informed if a
portion of a Company will be
received and cared for at the
barracks until the remainder
of a full Company is supplied
and whether in which event
a company thus formed will
be regarded the same with ref=
erence to the privilege of electing
its officers as if the whole number
were presented at once. The object
of submitting to you this question
is to provide against the diffi=
culty in retaining those we now have
for a few days until we obtain
the requisite number. An answer
by return mail will much oblige

Coll. F. Thomas   Yours Very
                                   S. S. Bennett

55

Hagerstown Aug. 10, 1861

Dr Sir

     I am requested to write you on behalf of the
residents of this place to be informed if a portion of a
Company will be received and cared for at the barracks
until the remainder of a full company is supplied and
whether which event a company thus formed will be
regarded the same with reference to the privilege of
electing its officers as if the whole number were presented
at once. The object of submitting to you this question is to
provide against the difficulty in recruiting those we now
have for a few days until we obtain the requisite number.
An answer by return mail will much oblige.

Yours Truly

J. D. Bennett

Hon F. Thomas

Hancock July 29th 1861

Dear Sir

I rec'd yesterday a number of hand bills
signed by the Sec. of War authorizing you to provide for
the organization of 4 regiments in your District
to protect the Canal &c & nearly all of [our] many who
have already expressed a willing ness to engage in such
service ask if Col. ____'s among regiments now raising
with its head quarters at Williams port is to be one
of them — Capt. Kennedy has been here sev-
eral times & will be again on the 5th of August next for the Co.
has obtained a considerable number already expects a large
number more & it is therefore important for the
interest of those who may be willing to aid in protecting the
Canal & to your purpose since we are alike that one be
informed of the subject in question — I have
therefore [reply] at your earliest Convenience —

I would like much to aid in the laudable
cause but am not able to endure much bodily labor
or stand marching — the office of Quarter master
would suit me — Could you or Col. you aid me in
obtaining the office for the Regiment nearest
here & [would] give satisfaction recommendation —
Mr. Francis Thomas   Yours very truly
                                      Jno. J. Thomas

57

Hancock July 24th 1861

Dear Sir

I rec'd. yesterday a number of handbills signed by the Sec'y of War authorizing you to provide for the organization of 4 regiments in your dist- to protect the Canal etc & nearly all of the many who have already expressed a willingness to engage in such service ask if Col. Lamon's regiment now raising with its headquarters at Williamsport is to be one of them. Capt. Kennedy has been here sev'l times & will be again on the 5th Aug next to recruit for the Col. has obtained a considerable number already & expects a large number more & it is therefor important for interests of those who may be willing to aid in protecting the Canal & to your purpose & success alike that we be informed of the subject in question. Please therefor reply at your earliest convenience.

I would like much to aid in the Laudable Cause but am not able to endure much bodily labor as hard walking, sir. The Office of Quartermaster would suit me. Could & would you aid me in obtaining the office for the regiment nearest here. I can give satisfactory recommendations.

Yours Very Truly
Jno. J. Thomas

Hon Francis Thomas

Hancock Md. August 5th 1861

Dear Sir

I will be in Hagerstown on the 7
inst, Wednesday, with a part and probably all
my company, ready to obey your orders. I have
100 names on my list, all but not less, three enlisted
but will be ready in four or five days. I think that
there is no doubt that I will be there with 75 good
horses. Let me know what I shall do with my men by
Wednesday mail at Hagerstown.

Yours &c. Respectfully
Lewis Dyche
Capt

To Major R. I. Smith of
United States Army
Frederick Md.

Hancock, Md. August 5th 1861

Dear Sir

I will be in Hagerstown on the 7 inst
Wensday with part and probably all my company ready to
obey your orders. I have 100 men on my list. All can not
leave their work now but will be ready in four of five days.
I think that there is no doubt that I will be there with 85
good men. Let me know what I shall do with my men by
Wensday mail at Hagerstown.

Yours Vy Respectfully
Lewis Dysche
Capt

To Major R. S. Smith of
United States Army
Frederick, Md.

New Hancock, Ind, August 16/61

Cal Col. Lewis Wallace
My Dear Sir

Since our return home
we have been laboring hard to raise another
Company full, but we find it difficult to get
83 men together at one time, and I fear we will
not be able to get them. Can not you devise
some way for us to get the number of men we have
now, mustered into Service (50) and give us the privilege
of recruiting afterwards to fill our Company.
Many of us feel extremely anxious to go into the
Service and should regret from the bottom of
our hearts should we fail. Hoping to hear from
you I remain

Your Obt My Respectfully
Geo S. Summers

near Hancock, Md Augus16/61

Ex Gov. Francis Thomas
My Dear Sir
Since our return home we
have been laboring hard to raise another Company full, but
we find it difficult to get 83 men together at one time and I
fear we will not be able to get them. Can not you devise
some way for us to get the number of men we have now,
mustered into Service (50) and give us the privelege of
recruiting afterwards to fill our Company. Many of us feel
extremely anxious to go into the Service and should repent
from the bottom of our hearts should we fail. Hoping to
hear from you
I remain
Yours Vy Respectfully
Geo. D. Summers

July 28th 1861
Millstone Point P.O.
Washington Co
Maryland

To the Hon. & Gov.
Francis Thomas

Sir Yesterday their arrived some
Hand bills. Setting fourth and
Order. Issued from Secatary of
War. Orthorising Gen to Organise
four Redgement Of Men as home
Gards. for the Protection Of Propert
&c. & Canall. to be compose from
Both side Of the Potomac, I wish
to know if they the Volenteers are
Subject to go to the Limits of
thos Counties mentine in begin
ing, if Call upon. or if they are
only bound to Serve along the
Potomac & Canall, as many think
they would be Compelled to go
as far as thos County extends
to defend. &c. further how they

how they are to be stationed
along the line wether in Maryland
or Virginia & how long they are to
inlist — wather equiped here or
at Frederick. and how many
of men must be raised for a Company
to be excepted. how, they are Paid
by the month or Quarterly & how
much per month. & how they are
to be Mustered into service Sworn
&c. & men that would inlist here
would they be sent any great
destant in the state of not any

please state all about the
Matter by return mail

Yours truly,
Jacob Myers
J M

Gov. F. Thomas

A Company will be raised
here less than ten days
Certain.

Yours J. Rogers

July 28th 1861
Millstone Point P.O.
Washington Co.
Maryland

To the Hon Ex Gov.
        Francis Thomas

Sir. Yesterday their arrived some handbills setting fourth
and order from Secretary of War orthorising four regiment
of men as home gards for the protection of property etc. &
canal to be compose from both sides of the Potomac. I
wish to know if they the volunteers are subject to go to the
limits of thoes counties mentune in Virginia, if call upon, or
if they are bound to serve along the Potomac and Canal, as
many think they would be compelled to go as far as thoes
county extends to defend & further how they know they
are to be stationed along the line wether in Maryland or
Virginia & how long they are to inlist & wether equiped
here or at Frederick and how many men must be raise for a
company to be excepted how they are paid by the month or
quarterly & how much per month & how they are to be
mustered into service sworn etc & men that would inlist
here would they be sent any grate distant in the state.
        Please state all about the matter by return mail.
                    Yours Truly
Ex Gov F. Thomas   Jacob Myers Jr

(P. S.) A company will be raise here less than ten days certain

Aug 5 1861 Millstone Point
Washington Co Md

To H. Hon Ex Gov Francis Thomas
Frederick City Md

Dear Sir I beg you to Excuse me to you, as to
Raising the Home guards and Hartisfied.
and further wish to Persue or for giving in
Information on the following Matter, in this that
our Company has been to raise to about 50
Men, that will swear into service, but the
amount of 83 required we cant raise, under
the Present circumstances, and our men
are not willing to Join in a Hancock Company,
upon the act of the Officers, which our men
Rather claim, as our Company is Larger
in numbers, the same case with the
the 3 Companies in Hancock they cant agree
in the same Matter, and neither company
can raise the 83 without Joining together
Now I wish to know if our Company
of about 50 Cnld not organise and
be equiped or Sworn in, and then come
back and Recruit until the No is equiped
for which we all are Satisfied could then
be easely to raise by so doing otherwise
I fear, our company will take to pieces and
the most of men has agreed to Join in with
Others, will you please write me Immediatly,
as we are in great Suspence,
Yours Verry
Mr F Thomas Esq   Jacob Kaya &c

Aug't 5 1861 Millstone Point
Washington Co. Md.

To the Hon Ex Gov Francis Thomas
Frederick City, Md.

Dear Sir. I rec'd your letter & paper in regard to raising
the Home Guards, and thankfull And further wish to
prevail on you giving us information on the following
matter- tis this that our company here can be raised to
about 50 men, that will sware into the service, but the
amount of 83 required we cant raise under the present
circumstances, and our men are not willing to join in a
Hancock Company upon the act of the Officers, which our
men rather claim, as our company is larger in members.
The same case with the 3 companies in Hancock they cant
agree in the same matter and wether company can raise the
83 without joining together. Now I wish to know if our
company of about 50 could not organis and be equiped &
sworn in, and then come back and recruit until the no's
required for which we all are satisfied could then be only be
raised by so doing. Otherwise I fear, our company will
toter to pieces and the most of the men here refuse to join
in with others. Will you please write me immediately as we
are in grate suspence.

Yours Truly

Mr F Thomas Esq   Jacob Myers Jr

Reihersville July 30th/61

Hon Francis Thomas,
                    Sir
                         Having noticed in the
Baltimore papers that you have permission from
the secretary of war to raise a brigade of volunteers
as Home Guard for the protection of western
Maryland & part of Virginia, and for particulars
to address you in Frederick, I wish to know
the particulars in regard to the forming of a
company the number requisite &c. I have a company organized and officers commissioned by the
Gov 9th of March 60. but never received any arms.
The company number about 80 men, including officers & musicians
but if that number is not sufficient I will recruit to
the number required, I would also like to know
whether government will furnish the uniform &c.
Please address to me at Reihersville Wash Co Md
immediately and state full particulars,
                         Yours Resp Fly
                    Washington McCoy Captain

70

Rohrersville July 26th 1861

Hon Francis Thomas

Sir

Having noticed in the Baltimore
papers that you have permission from the secretary of war
to raise a brigade of volunteers as Home Guards for the
protection of western Maryland & part of Virginia and for
particulars to address you in Frederick I wish to know the
particulars in regard to the forming of a company the
number requisite. I have a company organized and officers
commissioned by the Gov 9th of March 60, but never
received any arms. The company numbers about 55 men
including officers & musicians but if that number is not
sufficient I will recruit to the number required. I would
also like to know whether government will furnish the
uniforms etc. Please address me at Rohrersville Wash. Co.
Md. immediately and state full particulars.

Yours Respectfully

Washington McCoy

Captain

Indian Spring P.O.

Washington County Maryland
To the Hon. Francis Thomas
Member of Congress. Dear sir
I See it announced that they
are four regiments of home brigades
to be raised to protect our public
works and other property and loyal
citizens &c My Son wishes a
Situation as Captain to raise a
Squad of men in our neighbour
hood I live Just half ways between
Hancock and Clear Spring only one
mile from the the Canol at licking
Creek My Son has been wanting to
Join the Federal Army but i would
rather he would be connected with
this home brigade

If you can give him an office
in this undertaking to silence
or keep down Secessionism
I will ensure he will be all
rite I wish you to send me
a detailed information on the
Subject
        Truly yours &c
            John T. Mason, of I.

    Direct to Indian Spring
            Washington Co
                        Md
____iel Mason is my Sons
____ame he is Just 21

Indian Spring PO

Washington County Maryland   (July 1861)

To the Hon. Francis Thomas
Member of Congress.   dear Sir

I see it announced that they are four regiments of home
brigades to be raised to protect our public works and other
property and loyal citizens etc. My son wishes a situation
as Captain to raise a squad of men in our neighborhood. I
live just half way between Hancock and Clearspring only
one mile from the canal at Licking Creek. My son has been
wanting to join the Federal Army but I would rather he
would be connected with his home brigade. If you can
give him an office in this undertaking to silence or break
down Secessionism I will ensure he will be all rite. I wish
you to send me a detailed information on the subject.
                    Truly Yours etc
                    John T. Mason

Direct to Indian Spring
          Washington Co.

Daniel Mason is my Sons name he is Just 21

Rohrersville
Washington Co Ind.
July 26, /61

Hon. J. Thomas
        Sir, perceiving
that there are several regiments of Guards to be raised under your auspices or supervision, allow me to offer
you my services in any capacity that may be beneficial
to the undertaking — I would
like to recruit a company.
Please give me such information as will put me on
the right track, and oblige
            Respectfully yours

                W. Law

Rohrersville

Washington Co Md.

July 26, 1861

Hon F. Thomas

Sir, Perceiving that there are several
regiments of guards to be raised under your auspices or
supervision, allow me to offer you my services in any
capacity that may be beneficial to the undertaking. I would
like to recruit a company. Please give me such information
as will put me on the right track, and oblige

Respectfully Yours

W. Laws

Sharpsburg July 25th 1861

Han Francis Thomas
        Dear Sir
                Your favour of
the 24th inst is before me and in reply
would say that your request will be
promptly attended to. Our citizens are
rapidly enroling themselves and by
tuesday next will have a company
raised ready to report themselves.
When fully organised to whom and
when shall they report.
                Respectfully Yours&c
                Augustus A Biggs

Sharpsburg July 25th 1861

Hon Francis Thomas
                Dear Sir

                            Your favor of the 24th inst is
before me and in reply would say your request will be
promptly attended to. Our citizens are rapidly availing
themselves and by tuesday next will have a company raised
to report themselves. When fully organized to whom and
where should they report.

                                Respectfully Yours I am
                                Augustin A. Biggs

Dear Sir   Cum? July 14. 1861

Having understood that
it is the intention of the Government
to call out several Regiments
from Maryland and in Conversation
with Capt Thomas Johns the army
remarking that while he never
would make application himself
yet he would not hesitate to
decline serving the Government
in the present Crisis. Capt Johns
is a regular graduate of West Point
and has in regular service the
principal part of his life previous
to his resignation. I have also
understood that one of the
Regiments is to be raised in
Allegany County. My opinion
is that if Johns is appointed
Colonel there would be no
difficulty in his raising it
as he is well known in the County
and has the entire confidence
of every one both as regards
his qualification and his loyalty
as there is not a more ardent and

79

uncompromising supporter of the
Government in the State. indeed his
whole soul seems to be enlisted in
its success. I think if you would
procure the appointment of Colonel
for him for the Regiment to be raised
in this County the Government would
not only secure the services of an
efficient experienced officer
but it would meet with the hearty
approval of every loyal man in it
Gov.r Francis Thomas   Yours &c resp.
   Washington   Robert. Read

R. Read
4/1

Dear Sir

Having understood that it is the intention of the Government to call out several regiments from Maryland and in conversation with Capt Thomas Johns this evening remarking that while he never would make application himself yet he would not hesitate to decline serving his government in the present crisis. Capt Johns is a regular graduate of West Point and was in regular service the principal part of his life previous to his resignation. I have also understood that one of the regiments is to be raised in Allegany County. My opinion is that if Johns is appointed Colonel there would be no difficulty in his raising it as he is well known in the County and has the entire confidence of every one both as regards his qualifications and his loyalty as there is not a more ardent and uncompromising supporter of the government in the state, indeed his whole soul seems to be enlisted in its success. I think if you would procure the appointment of Colonel for him for the regiment to be raised in this county the government would not only secure the services of an efficient experienced officer but it would meet with the hearty approval of every loyal man in it.

Yours Vy Resp
Robert Read

Gov Francis Thomas
    Washington

Cumberland July 25th 1861

Hon? Francis Thomas
                    My dear Sir
                              I have learned
to-day through Mr Robert Bruce, that
the government has determined
upon raising four regiments in
Maryland; and that arrangements
for the purpose of raising one
are, in some measure, con-
fided to you.
    I learn, it is expected that one
can be raised in this county.
    Of this, I make not the slightest
doubt.
    It is most important however,
to the success of the measure,
and to their usefulness afterwards,
that a competent man should
be put at the head of the regiment as Colonel.
    As soon as I heard of it, I ought

your procure, for Mr Wh... such a commission, as the most certain method of procuring a regiment here, composed of the best material.

It is not advisable to wait the raising of the regiments, before appointing the Colonel; but to make the appointments of a good man, in whom the people can have confidence, and they will then enroll.

Mr I... is a man, who has stood for the maintenance of the government, against all rebellion, and who has always been and is now, one of the outspoken union men.

It is also proper to state that Mr I... is a thorough military man, and a good disciplinarian.

I am sure I speak the sentiments of the entire community here on this subject. If it

an interview with Mr Thomas Johns,
who is a graduate of West-point,
and served in the Army for
many years, to ascertain whether
he would accept, at the hands
of the Secretary of war, a commission, as Colonel of a regiment to be raised. Mr Johns
replied that he never sought
any place or position in his life,
and would not now, but
was ready, if his country called
him, in this the hour of trouble,
to respond at once.
Mr Johns is as modest as he is
known to be brave; and as a
military man has the entire confidence of the people of this
county. If it were once known
that he had a commission as
Colonel, a regiment, in my
judgment, would rally
around him at once —
    I respectfully suggest, that

were known that Mr Wheas
would accept the place —
truly yours
Geo A Pearce

P.S. Please let me learn
from you in reply —
G.A.P.

T.A Pearce

Cumberland July 25th 1861

Hon'l Francis Thomas

My dear Sir

I have learned today through Mr. Robert Bruce that the government has determined upon raising four regiments in Maryland and that arrangements for the purpose of raising one are in some measure consigned to you.

I learn it is expected that one can be raised in this county. Of this I make not the slightest doubt.

It is most important however to the success of the measure and to their usefulness afterwards that a competent man should be put at the head of the regiment as Colonel.

As soon as I heard of it, I sought an interview with Mr. Thomas Johns who is a graduate of West Point and served in the Army for many years, to ascertain whether he would accept, at the hands of the Secretary of War, a commission as Colonel of a regiment to be raised. Mr Johns replied that he never sought any place of position in his life, and would not now, but was ready if his country called him in this hour of trouble, to respond at once. Mr Johns is respected and is known to be brave; and as a military man has the entire confidence of the people of this county. If it were once known that he had a commission as Colonel, a regiment, in my judgement, would rally around him at once.

86

I respectfully suggest that you procure for Mr. Johns such a commission, as the most certain method of procurring a regiment here composed of the best material.

It is not undesirable to await the raising of the regiment before appointing the Colonel, but to make the appointment of a good man, is when the people can have confidence and they will then enroll.

Mr Johns is a man who has stood for the maintenance of the government, against all rebellion, and who has always been and is now, one of the outspoken loyal men.

It is also proper state that Mr Johns is a thorough military man, and a good disciplinarian. I am sure I speak the sentiments of the entire community her on this subject, if it were known that Mr. Johns would accept the place.

Truly Yours
Geo. A. Pierce

P.S.

please let me hear from you in reply.

Sharpsburg Washington C[ounty] Md.
August 7th 1861

To Hon. Francis Thomas M.C.

Dear Sir

The Sharpsburg Riflemen under
my command, a company which has the honor
of being, I believe, the only regularly organized
company in this county, have recruited our
ranks to about seventy, all anxious to
get into the service immediately. And I
write for the purpose of ascertaining from
you whether it is possible or not for the
Company to be mustered into service as a
company, with a few less than the number
specified, and with permission to fill the
ranks afterwards, which I am fully satisfied
will not require more than a week or ten days.

Have the goodness to write me at your
earliest convenience, and oblige

Your Obd't Serv't
William B. Cook
1st Sharpsburg Riflemen

Sharpsburg, Washington Co, Md.
August 7th 1861

Hon. Francis Thomas M.C.

Dear Sir

The "Sharpsburg Rifles"
under my command, a company which has the honor, I
believe, of being the only regularly organized company in
this county, have recruited our ranks to about seventy, all
anxious to get into the service immediately. And I write
for the purpose of ascertaining from you whether it is
possible or not for the company to be mustered into service
as a company with a few less than the number specified,
and with permission to fill the ranks afterwards, which I am
fully satisfied will not require more that a week or ten days.

Have the goodness to write me at your earliest
convenience, and oblige.

Your Obdt. Sevt.
R. Ellsworth Cook
Capt. Sharpsburg Rifles

Sharpsburg Washington Co
Augt 8th 1861

Dear Sir

I wrote you yesterday
directed to Washington in regard to regard to
the Company (the Sharpsburg Rifles) were
raised at this place. I wished to know
what Course I should pursue to have the
company mustered into service. Our ranks
are full, the officers elected. But the men
are considerably scattered and am fearful
that I could not collect them to a man so
as to march them to Fred'k, without exception
and what I wished to know is whither we
could be mustered in as a company with
less than what is required by law, with permission to fill the ranks to that number as they
come in. If this privilege is allowed I do not
do it I my ability to increase the company
to even 100 men — And as I conceive that
it would be exceedingly hard asking if this

90

Congressional District should fulfill do
her duty, in furnishing the troops for home
protection, even should Virginia neglect
or refuse to respond. As I am a stranger
to you I would respectfully refer you as
reference to Col. Jno Miller & A. A. Biggs
or Levin Fenton of the place; with whom
I believe there can be no question of loyalty—

    Have the goodness to let me hear from
you in reference to this matter at your
earliest convenience

                Very Respectfully
                your Obedient Servant
                R. Ellsworth Cook

Hon Francis Thomas
Fred^k Maryland

Sharpsburg, Washington Co. Md.

August 8th 1861

Dear Sir

I wrote you yesterday directed to Washington in regard to regards to the Company (the Sharpsburg Rifles) now raised at this place. I wished to know what course I should persue to have the Company mustered into service. Our ranks are full, the officers elected. But the men are considerably scattered, and am fearful that I could not collect them to a man so as to march them to Fred'k. without exceptions; and what I wished to know is whether we could be mustered in as a company with a few less than the 83 what is required by law, with permission to fill the ranks to that number as they come in. If this privelege is allowed, I do not doubt my ability to increase the company to over 100 men - and must confess that it would be extremely humiliating if this Congressional District should fail to do her duty in furnishing the troops for home protection, even should Virginia neglect or refuse to respond. As I am a stranger to you, I would respectfully refer you as reference to Col. Jno. Miller, Dr. AA Biggs, or Sevin Jenson of this place; with whom I believe there can be no question of loyalty.

Have the goodness to let me hear from you in reference to this matter at your earliest convenience.

Very Respectfully

Your Obedient Servant

R. Ellsworth Cook

Hon Francis Thomas
    Fred'k. Maryland

Weverton Med, July 26, 1861

Hon. F. Thomas.

Sir.

I want some information in forming
a company to compose the four Regiments
in Virginia. The Lovettsville company
of the fifty Sixth Regiment of the 6th
Brigade and 2d Division Virginia
Militia. is in Weverton now and she
wants to form our Selves in a company
and get armed from the government
and Return to Loudon County Virginia
a gane and Twin these Regiments which
is to be a raised ther. We hate to leve
our homes and our Fathers and all
our relitives ther and Since we have left
the Rebbs is ruining our Parents for
Gods Sake helpt us to come So that
we may return to our County and
keep them down we can raise a
company in a day if you will get us
armes So that we can return a gane
We do not want to Twin the Regiments in
Maryland but these in Virginia to protect
our homes, I want you to give me all the
information you can on this subject also
wether we can organize her and then return

to virginia & if the we must organize
in virginia, If we can get armes [?] and
and then return to virginia I hope you
will fix every thing for us so that we [?]
my return home & gave We left for this
reason because we did not go for the [?]
but to go for the government Please [answer]
this by the next mail I am a [Lieutenant]
in this company commissioned by John [?]

Your obedient Servant
Luther H. [?]

Direct your Letter Warrenton
N. C.

Weverton Md July 25th 1861
Hon F. Thomas.
Sir.

I wont Som information on those forming a company to compose thes four Regiments in Virginia, The Lovittsville Company of the fifty Sixth Regiment of the 6th Brigade and 2't Division Virginia Militia is in Weverton now and we wonto form our Selves in a company and get arms form the goverment and return to Loudon County Virginia a gane and join thes Regiment which is to be raised ther. We had to lieve our homes and our Fathers and all our relitives ther and sense we hav left the Rebles is runing over our Parents For Gods Sake help us get some armes so the we may return to our County and keep them down We can raise a company in a day if you will get us armes so that we can return a gane We do not wonto join the Regiments in Maryland but thes in Virginia to protect our homes. I want you to give me all the information you can on this subject also wether we can organize her and then return to Virginia or wether we must organize in Virginia, if we can get armes her and then return to Virginia I hope you will fix every thing for us so that we may return home a gane We left for this reason becus we did not go for the South but we go for the goverment. Please answer this by the next mail I am in Lewistown in this county Commissioned by John Letorze

Your obedient Servant
Luther W. Potterfield
Direct your letter Weverton Md

95

Martinsburg Va July 2nd 1861

To Hon Francis A. Thomas

Dear Sir

Haveing seen an advertisment in the Baltimore papers for the organization of A Home Guard in several of the Counties in virginia I have been requested to write to you to know full particulars in regards to the Case there is A number of men in this place who are desirous of forming A Home Guard providing they Could be sustained and furnished with arms and A great meny of them think that the Advertisment in the paper is untrue I think if you would send A written Certificate to that effect that there will be no diffaculty in forming A very large Company in this

96

Town I have taken it upon my
self to write you and I shall
use every exersion to raise &c
and as meny more as possible
Answer immediately and you will
confer A reciprocal favor on
     Your Obedient Servant
     Wm H. Wright
Martinsburg Berkeley County Virginia

Martinsburg Va. July 26th 1861

To Hon Francis A. Thomas
                    Dear Sir
                    Having see an advertisment in the
Baltimore papers for the organization of A Home Guard in
Several of the Counties in Virginia I have been requested
to write to you to know full particulars in regards the case
there is a number of men in this place who are desirous of
forming A Home Guard providing thay could be Sustained
and furnished with arms and a great meny of them think the
addvertisment in the paper is untrue. I think if you would
send a written cirtificate to that effect that there will be no
diffaculty in forming A very large company in this town I
have taken it apon myself to write you and I shall use every
exersion to raise A Co and as meny more as possible
Answer immediately and you will confer A receprocal
favor on
                    Your Obedient Servant
                    Wm H. Wright

Martinsburg - Berkely County Virginia

Maj. R. S. Smith
            Fredk, Md.

Sir.
        I hereby report to you.
that a Volunteer Company has
this day been organized in this
City, under the authority given
by Secretary Cameron to Wor, Hamis
Thomas. for the protection of the
Canal &c The Company Consist
of One hundred & one men, including
Company officers
        The officers are
                            H. Kesley Capt.
                            Jas. C. Lyons 1st Lieut
                            Geo. Cooter 2 .
                            Geo Wigley 1st Sergt.
                            Saml Shipley 2 .
                            Lloyd Bowder 3 "
                            Levi Shaw 4.
                            Wr Johnson 5 .

Gov Thomson informs me
that from the date of the report
to you of the organization. the pay
of the Volunteers commences.

We are destitute of the means
of Subsistence. Clothing. Arms &c.
but hope that we will soon
be furnished with them.

There is a very fair prospect of
raising 6 or 7 Companies, varying
from 83 to 101 Men in the next ten
days—

Very Respectfully Your
Bruce Resley
Capt.

Cumberland
August 12. 1861.

Maj. R. S. Smith
            Fred'k. Md.
Sir

I hereby report to you that a Volunteer Company
has this day been organized in this City, under the authority
given by secretary Cameron to Hon Francis Thomas for the
protection of the Canal etc. The company consists of one
hundred & one men including officers.

The officers are	H. Resley Capt.		
	Jam C. Lynn	1st Leut	
	Geo Cooter	2	"
	Geo Wigley	1st Sergt	
	Saml Shipley	2	"
	Lloyd Dowden	3	"
	Levi Shaw	4	"
	W. Johnson	5	"

Gov Warren informs me that from the date of the report to
you of the organization, the pay of the volunteers
commences. We are destitute of the means of subsistence,
clothing, arms, etc. but hope that we will soon be furnished
with them. There is a very fair prospect of raising 6 or 7
companies varying from 83 to 101 men in the next ten
days.

                    Very Respectfully yours
                    Horace Resley
                        Capt.

Cumberland
        August 12, 1861

Cumberland, Md.
August 15. 1861.

Hav Francis Thomas,
     Frederick Md.
                    Sir,
                          I hereby
report to you the recruiting and
organization of a Company numbering one hundred men, for the purpose of being mustered into the
Service of the U. States, as a part
of the Brigade now being formed
on the border line of Maryland &
Virginia. The officers Elected
are— James D. Roberts, Captain
        John Irvine 1st Lieutenant
        James A. Morrow 2nd Lieutenant,
And I report the Company ready
to be mustered into service at any
time you may find it con-

venient to do so.
Respectfully,

[signature] Captn.

Cumberland, Md.
August 15. 1861

Hon Francis Thomas
Frederick, Md.

Sir;

I hereby report to you the recruiting and organization of a company numbering one hundred men, for the purpose of being mustered into the service of the U. States, as a part of the Brigade now being formed on the border line of Maryland & Virginia-
James D. Roberts, Captain

John Irvine 1st Lieutenant
James A Morrow 2nd Lieutenant

And I report the Company ready to be mustered into service at any time you may find it convenient to do so.

Respectfully,
James D. Roberts Captain

Cumberland Office 16th August 1861

Maj. R. S. Smith

Dr Sir

The Company known as the
"... Union Fencibles" was duly organized
this day numbering 101 men for the Home Brigade
by electing the following Officers viz.
Capt. ...., 1st Lieut. ..... Bryan
2nd Lieut. ..... Mahaney, we ask acceptance
and desire information how to further proceed

Yours truly
....

P.S. We can send the Roll if desired. I wish you would
send me any blanks you think I may need

Cumberland Md 16th August 1861

Maj R. S. Smith

        Sir,

           The Company known as the "McClelland Union Invincibles" was duly organized this day numbering 101 men, for the Home Brigade by electing the following Officers *viz*

       Capt Chas G. McClelland, 1st Lieut Robt Cowan, 2nd Lieut Lloyd McHaney. We ask acceptance and desire information how to further proceed.

              Yours Truly

               Chas G. McClelland

P.S. We can send the Roll if desired. I wish you would send any blanks you think I need

Frostburg, Md, Aug. 6, 1861

Hon. Francis Thomas,

    Dr. Sir,

        In obedience
to the Call of the Hon. Sec. of War, made through
you, the writer has raised a company of Volunteers
subject to the requirements of said Call, and is
ready to meet you personally or by proxy
in Cumberland at an early day to be mustered
into service— The men are anxious to be out
early— Will you please inform me at your
earliest convenience when I shall be in Cumberland
with my men; Whether they must undergo a Medical
examination; To whom must I report; When the
Company will be received into service, and all other
information necessary for immediate reception—
    If it were known who the field Officers were to
be, more could be obtained— How do Company
officers to be examined by Military Board! —
    Please inform me early—
        Truly Yours
           John H. Huntley
           Capt.

Frostburg, Md. August 6, 1861

Hon Francis Thomas,

                Dear Sir,

                        In obedience to the call of
the Hon Sec. of War made through you, the writer has
raised a company of volunteers subject to the requirements
of said call, and is ready to meet you personally or by
proxy in Cumberland at an early day to be mustered into
service_ The men are anxious to be out early_ Will you
please inform me at your earliest convenience when I shall
be in Cumb'd with my men; whether they must undergo a
medical examination; to whom must I report; when the
Company will be received into service, and all other
information necessary for immediate reception.

        If it were known who the field officers were to be,
more could be obtained_ Have the Company officers to be
examined by Military Board?

        Please inform me early_

                Truly Yours

                    John H. Huntley

                        Capt.

Frostburg Aug 16th 1861

R. S. Smith
      Maj. U. S. A.
            Dr Sir
                  Your favor of the 16th
rec'd — I have the honor to inform you that we
to day organized and elected Officers.
      Eighty six men were enrolled
      Within three or four days, we expect to
have fifteen or twenty more men —
      the letter directed to Gov. Thomas was
written by my request, during my absence,
by my Father —
                        truly Yours
                        Capt Jno. H. Huntley
P.S.
      As some of my men live at a distance
from the place where organized, I have
seen proper to quarter them at Frostburg

Frostburg Aug16th1861

RS Smith
      Maj. U. S. A.
        Dr Sir
           Your favor of the 10th recd. I have the honor to inform you that we today organized and elected Officers.

Eighty-six men were enrolled. Within three or four days, we expect to have fifteen or twenty more men_

The letter directed to Gov. Thomas was written by my request, during my absence, by my Father.

        Truly Yours
        Capt John H. Huntley

P. S.

As some of my men live at a distance from the place where organized, I have seen proper to quarter them at Frostburg.

111

Lonaconing Maryland August 13th 1861

Major R. S. Smith
    Frederick, Md.

        Sir

            I have a company here of
between 80 and 100 men, on the 7th of this month we
organized and I now report to you and await your
instructions. Many of the men are from a distance and I
should like them mustered in as soon as possible as it is a
great deal of trouble & expense for me to keep them
together.

      Hoping to hear from you soon, I am

                Your Obt Ser

                Alex Shaw Capt

Emmittsburg Maryland August 14th 1851

Gov. Thomas
Frederick

Sir —

I have reported an Company of Volunteers 80 to 100 Men to Maj Smith, and hope to hear from him soon, as I am anxious to have them sworn in so as to be relieved of the expense & trouble of keeping them together —

I may lose some of my Men as the Canal is about to commence, but bring the case could be met the occasion with 60 or 70 Men, from those present till my Company was filled up. Many of our Miners are on the Rail Roe [Rail Road?] required, and would be glad to go with the Army, but will not come back till the Company has been accepted. Will you have the kindness to inform me about this? If I could have an answer before the Company is sworn [is accepted for] I will continue loose some of my Men, and if I can not get on with less than 85 I may have to give up.

Hoping to hear from you soon I remain

Your Obd't Ser't

Lonaconing Maryland August 14th 1861

Gov Thomas
Frederick

   Sir

    I have reported a Company of between
80 & 100 men to Maj Smith, and hope to hear from him
soon as I am anxious to have them sworn in so as to be
relieved of the expense and trouble of keeping them
together.

    I may lose some of my men as the Canal is about to
be opened. Such being the case, could I not be received
with 60 or 70 men, and then recruit til my company has
filled up. Many of our miners are in the BrodLet region,
and would be glad to go into the service, but will not come
back til the Company has been accepted. Will you have the
kindness to inform me about this? If work here is resumed
before the company is called for, I will certainly lose some
of my men, and if I can not get in with less than 83 I may
have to give up.

    Hoping to hear from you soon, I remain
        Y Obt. Svt.
        Alex Shaw

Clearspring August 3d 1861

Maj. Smith

Dear Sir I
received a note from the Hon. J. Thomas
stating that any information required
in regard to the organization of the Home
Brigade you would furnish him

I organized a Cavalry Company
here under the State Militia law
three months ago & have been commissioned by the Gov. & sworn in with the
expectation of getting arms from the
State but fail in that, I then made
an effort to procure arms from the
government & I fear will meet with
the same fate. I do not hesitate in
saying that my Company consists of
the best men in the district all farmers
& mechanics, men too who have a good deal
at stake & are willing to defend their property, with all others who may be attacked,
we do not ask the Gov. to furnish us
with anything but arms, we will uniform
& equip this horse, & I think that we
are entitled to have some chance for
arms, we do not ask for more than sword
& breech loading Carbine. I do not know
if the Company will attach itself to any of
the Reg'ts but will say that we will
act at all times with them when ever
needed, we do not ask pay only when in
service. please give this your early
attention & oblige

L R Cushwa
Capt of Cavalry

Clearspring August 3d 1861

Maj Smith

Dear Sir I received a note from
the Hon F. Thomas stating that any information required in
regard to the organization of the Home Brigade you would
furnish it.

I organized a Cavalry Company here under the State
Militia Law three months ago & have been commissioned
by the Gov'r & sworn in with the expectation of getting
arms from the State, but fail in this. I then made an effort
to procure arms from the Government & I fear will meet
with the same fate. I do not hesitate in saying that my
Company consists of the best men in the district all farmers
and mechanics; men too who have a good deal at stake &
are willing to defend their property with all others who may
be attacked. We do not ask the Govt to furnish us with
anything but arms, the men will uniform and equip their
horses & I think that we are entitled to have some chance
for arms, we do not ask for more than swords and breech
loading carbines. I do not know if the company will attach
itself to any of the Regts but will say that we will act at all
times with them when ever needed. We do not ask pay
only when in service! Please give this your early attention
& oblige.

J. R. Cashour
Capt of Cavalry

Sharpsburg Aug't 17th 1861

R. S. Smith Esq
Mag. U. S. A.

Sir

your favor of the request of Gen Sherman dated July 8
Send. Army Stated &c

With regard to the officers
can say nothing of significance, each
severally, is, are all such officers to be
put to the expense and paid or
given their private service or to another
furnished them, by Government, in equipment
of the force raised in your district

I would like to know a copy of the
form of Oath entitling the sureties, so
they may be bound up by signing a
bond here

Or me hear from holders & drive
soon, oblige yours

E. B. Keen

P.S. in speaking of equipment I can reference
use to you, of their equipment, some speak privately
their own & ours, other who to the said I know
be furnished in due time by Government, or ......

Sharpsburg Augst 17th 1861

R. S. Smith Esqr
    Maj. USA

        Dr Sir

               Yours forwarded by request of
Gov. Thomas come duly to hand. Pay stated etc.

    With regard to the officers, you say nothing of
equipments, rations, servants, etc. Are all such expenses to
be met by the officers and paid out of their own private
purce or is anything furnished them by government
independent of the pay named in your statement. I would
like to have a coppy of the form of oath binding the
members so they may be bound up by signing a list here.
let me hear from by return of mail please & oblige.

               Yours

                  E. W. Knode

P.S. in Speaking of equipments I have refference also to
horse & their equipment. Some speak furnishing their own
horses, others who do not will I presume be furnished in
due time by government.   Yours Truly

Baltimore Aug 4th/62

Capt J. S. Yellett,

Dear Sir.

I am under the necessity of writing you again. Not have received any reply to my last note and request you to remit me the am't of my bill for flags. As I called on Mr Burnham. Until I am tired and I cant get any money. Your Early atten tion to this will greatly Oblidge me As flags are always Cash

Yours Respectfully
O. Herring
per L.S.H.

Baltimore Aug 4th /62

Capt J. I. Yellett
     Dear Sir.

     I am under the necessity of writing you again.
Not have received any reply to my last note and request to
you to remit the amt of my bill for flags. As I called on the
Mr. Burnham. I cant get any money. Your early attention
to this will greatly oblige me as flags are always cash.

          Yours Respectfully
           O. Herring
             per S. E. H.

PART III
AFTER THE LETTERS

As noted, the above documents are in the possession of the author. In researching the subject of the recruitment of the Potomac Home Brigade, the author was fortunate to discover a number of very useful and interesting collateral documents in the archives of the Historical Society of Frederick County. The following is a letter from Francis Thomas to Lieutenant-Colonel Dennis.

Browns Hotel
Sept 16 / 61

Dear Sir
  The Administration has acted kindly in the affair that caused me great uneasiness. Having urged the military officers gather of which you are, with others, commanders. I felt great solicitude while there was danger that the best of these Volunteers might be placed in imcompetant hands. And I was mortified too, at the prospect of seeing all my ulterior purposes frustrated by the appointment of a Commander in Chief altogether disqualified. All is now right. *Edward O. Cresap Ord has been appointed Brigadier General with the understanding that he is to command the Potomac Home Brigade. Gen. Ord was born in Allegany County and is a lineal descendant of one of the Cresaps who was so much distinguished in the border wars before and during the Revolution. He is now about forty two years of age was educated at West Point and is an accomplished and brave soldier.*

The thousand guns with accutrements will leave
here tomorrow via Rail Road for Frederick. Please take
care that they do not fall into enemies hands if anything
unforseen occurs.

> *Yours Respectfully*
> *Francis Thomas*

Col G. R. Dennis

Ord was a Captain of Artillery at the time of his
appointment to Brigadier General on September 14, 1861.
He graduated from the U. S. Military Academy in 1839,
seventeenth in a class of thirty-one.

The next letters were found in the Papers of Colonel
Maulsby.

> *Hagerstown Sept 6, 1861*

Dear Col
Mr. Daniel Mumma of this town requests me to
submit his name and that of Wm Johnston of Fredk County
to you as applicants for the appointment of Subtlers to the
Home Brigade. I know Mr. Mumma to be a staunch active
Unionist.
I regret to say that I have neither see nor heard of
the Gov. or the Major since the receipt of your favor upon
the subject of recruiting. If we had a portion of that
money we could soon fill up your Regt you can be assured.

> *Yours Truly*
> *J. D. Bennett*

A notation on the reverse reads: *J. D. Bennett*
Mumma Sept 11, 1861 sent check $50

On September 11, Bennett replied to Lt. Colonel
Dennis.

Hagerstown Sept 11, 1861

Dear Sir
I have the pleasure of acknowledging the receipt of
your favor of Yesterday in which you enclosed me a check
on the Central Bank of Frederick for $50. to defray
expenses on recruiting for the 1st Regt of the Md. Home
Brigade which I will endeavor to use to the best advantage
and account to you for by receipts. I herewith return you
the receipts for $50. with my signature as your requested.
Respectfully your
Obnt Servt
J. D. Bennett
Lt. Col G. R. Dennis

The following letter is from Lieutenant I. M. Martin
to Colonel Maulsby.

Hagerstown, Sept 23rd 1861

Col Molsby
Dear Sir
I called on Mr Bennett and he stated that he had
expended all the funs he had to myself, Burck & Calkisher
for recruiting purposes and requested me to write the sum
to you which he will furnish receipts for by Tuesday mail.

I am here now and would like to do all the service for the country I possibly can. And as I have spent considerable of my own money you will greatly oblige me by sending to Mr Bennett a draft so I can continue recruiting this week. Please send it by return mail.

A, B, I send 12 recruits to day by Millers Buss

Capt Yontz will hand you this
Very Respectfully
Lt. I. M. Martin

Francis Thomas wrote the following to Colonel Maulsby.

August 31, 1861

Dear Sir

Allow me to ask you to recollect that I am entitled to fifty five dollars on account of that sum placed in your hands, and to $350. on account to that sum paid to Mr. Boyd for Indian blankets to be returned out of the first monthly payment to our Volunteers.

In mustering in the companies & Regiments great care ought to be taken to secure to the volunteers the right to serve on the Southern boundary of Maryland and nowhere else. If mustered in generally we may have difficulty here after.

Please say to Major Smith that he did not return to me the original letter of Secy Cameron, on which is an endorsement of President Lincoln, authorizing me to raise the Brigade.

Yours Respectfully
Francis Thomas

Col W. P. Maulsby

On September 2, 1861, Governor Thomas wrote the following to Colonel Maulsby:

Cumberland
Sept 2, 1861

Dear Sir
    Col Thomas Johns and myself intend to leave this place day after tomorrow for Washington City to make some arrangements as to the companies mustered in here. During my stay in Washington I wish to make such arrangements as may be necessary for the efficiency and comfort of the Regiment under your command and wish, for that purpose, to have from yourself or Major Smith, <u>full minutes</u> and particular information, as to the number of Companies, the number of Cavalry Companies, representation of the condition of the Volunteers at Frederick, and of their wants, equipment, canvass, cam(p) equipage clothing, etc. as will enable to see what ought to be and can be done, at Washington by me in their behalf.
    Please direct your letter to the care of the Mr Brown, at whose Hotel I propose to stay.
                     Yours Respectfully
                     Francis Thomas

The following document was found in the papers of Colonel Maulsby at the Frederick County Historical Society. It is an unsigned, undated memorandum outlining the policies and procedures for recruiting volunteers. Having read a number of papers written by Maulsby, it is the author's supposition that this document is in his hand.

I or any officers including officers not mustered in have power to enroll & accept any number of men over half a company. The pay of men commences on the day they are accepted. So soon as the company is filled it may be mustered in. Officers already accepted can recruit & enroll the men recruited at the place where enrolled. The enrollment consists of a company book in which the exact names are entered, with the date of each man's enrollment, with a statement of the number of miles to Frederick, the place of rendevous. At same time make a description in same book stating place of enrollment, birth, age, height, color of eyes & hair. The book must be ruled in columns for these purposes. At the time of enrollment each man can be sworn in by a magistrate. The recruit receives 2 1/2 (cents) per mile from place of enrollment to rendevous.

The technical first mustering in of a company consists of making out a triplicate Muster Roll, one copy to be retained at Regimental Head Quarters, one to be sent to Division Head Quarters, one to be sent to Adjutant General. This Muster Roll is to be certified by the Capt. & by the Mustering Officer, whether Volunteer already in,

or by Regular Army Officer. On this roll all pay &
allowances are based.

     Blankets and part of clothing are to be paid for out
of $3.50.

     Recruits enrolled by accepted officers, not for
particular companies receive pay from time of enrollment.

     Any man desiring to recruit a company may enroll
men in manner before stated & each man as soon as
enrolled will be entitled to pay so soon as 1/2 a co. is
recruited. The officers may be elected & mustered in &
the Co. carry on until filled.

     In correspondence with Departments observe rules
in Army Regulations.

     An oath of allegiance was required of all recruits and
was to be administered no more than six days after
enlistment. Lord's <u>They Fought for the Union</u> provides the
text of the mandatory oath: *I _____, do solemnly swear*
or affirm (as the case may be) that I will bear true
allegiance to the United States of America, and that I will
serve them honestly and faithfully against all their
enemies or opposers whatsoever, and observe and obey
the orders of the President of the United States, and the
orders of the officers appointed over me, according to the
rules and articles for the government of the armies of the
United States.

     When the first call for volunteers was promulgated,
a large number of boys as young as fourteen and older men
up to the age of sixty-two enlisted. At first surgeons made
only a cursory examination of recruits and as a
consequence, a large percentage became ill, entered the

hospitals, and either died or were given medical discharges. Many concealed illness or infirmity in their enthusiasm to enter the ranks. In about mid 1862 the minimum age of a recruit was set at eighteen years, and the maximum age was forty-five. Those between eighteen and twenty-one had to have the signed permission of their fathers in order to enlist. The doctors were also much more fastidious in their examinations of enlistees; although, it was said that as long as a volunteer had at least two opposable front teeth to bite open the paper cartridges and an index finger with which to pull the trigger, he would probably not be rejected. The exceptions to this were obvious drunkenness, physical infirmities, or observable mental retardation or dementia.

The recruits who volunteered for enlistment in the Potomac Home Brigade were enrolled for three years or the duration of the War, whichever ended sooner. After half of a company had been mustered in, the first lieutenant of the company could then be sworn in. When a sufficient number had been enrolled to fill the company, the second lieutenant and the captain were mustered into service. Upon the completion of four companies, the lieutenant colonel would be mustered in, and the major was enrolled after six companies were filled. The colonel, adjutant, quartermaster, surgeon, assistant surgeon, and the chaplain were required to await the completion of the entire regiment before being mustered in. The regiment then went into camp and commenced training. In the case of the First Regiment, its bivouac site was Camp Worman.

Doctor Lewis Steiner wrote this letter to Colonel Maulsby after inspecting Camp Worman for the Sanitary Commission.

Frederick City Sept 18, 1861

Col W. P. Maulsby
1st Regt. Home Brigade

Sir

Having made a hasty inspection of your camp, in accordance with orders of the Sanitary Comm., I take the liberty of directing your attention to the condition of the privies used by the men under your command. One of the causes of camp-dysentary and low forms of disease in camp is the condition of the pits used for the collection of the soldiers' urine and excrements. The gases, proceding from there, contaminate the air so as to produce serious injuries to the constitutions of those obliged to inhale it and serves to prepare them for reception of any disease incident to the locality. On this account the Sanitary Commission are desirous that the Army Regulations, with reference to the construction and management of sinks should be adopted in our army, and that the use or ordinary privies be given up. Such sinks are readily filled in from day to day with earth, and thus prevented from becoming offensive.

With sentiments of high esteem
I have the honor to be
Yr Obedient Servant
Lewis H. Steiner
Sanitary Inspector

The next letter is also in the Maulsby Papers.

Philadelphia Pa
Sept 6th 1861

Col Maulsby
Dr Sir

Mr. Blocher and Capt. Faithful has been talking to me about recruiting a Band for your Regiment. By their request I went to Frederick to see you to asertain the peticulars. What the inducements were, what rules the Band would be subject to, their pay etc., but as you were not at home I failed to get to see you. Mr Blocher introduced me Gen Shrimer, but he could not give me any information, and referred me to Mr. Doll, he gave me the prices correctly with the exception of the pay of the leader which is the same as the 2nd Lieutenant which I have asertained since, if I should go into it I would not have any but fine performers and men of good moral character. But I could not enlist such at government rates. If you will do as the Northern Regiments do all the commissioned officers contribute monthly so much to the support of the Band. I will take hold of it. Say one hundred dollars monthly beside the goverment pay. With that inducement I can enlist quite a number of the Blues Band of Balto. a band of 15 or 18 would be plenty large enough. Please answer this as soon as practicable. I have the same inducement offered by an Indiana Regiment but I would greatly prefer attaching myself to a Reg. of my native state.

direct to 42 Lexington St. Baltimore as I will be home in 3
or 4 days.

Truly Yours

J. Mortimer Hurley

Teacher of Music

The Superintendent of the Northern Central
Railway, in reply to Lieutenant-Colonel Dennis, wrote this
letter on Company letterhead:

NORTHERN CENTRAL RAILWAY,

Superintendent's Office, Calvert Station,

Baltimore, Sept 24th 1861

Col Geo R Dennis

Frederick

Md

*Your favour of 21st requesting us to furnish
transportation for recruits for the Potomac Home Brigade
duly received and will be promptly honored I furnished
transportation to Mr Loyd, who was represented by Mr D.
Blocher to be one or your recruiting officers*

Very Respectfully

& Truly Yours

Jas C Clark

Supt

Maulsby's head of recruiting in Baltimore was Daniel
Blocher. On September 24 he wrote to Lieutenant-Colonel
Dennis the following:

132

Balt Sept 24th 61

Col G. R. Dennis

Dear Sir

The cars failing to make a connexion on Saturday I did not reach Washington. But on going to the Fountain ascertained that Col. Spates was there and would see Gov. Thomas. Today he returned and informed me that he had an interview with Gov. T. and also with Gen. Scott & Mr. Blair. That the whole matter has been postponed for a time, and that he has a hope that things will yet turn out right. Mr B's position is just now rather peculiar on account of the Freemont difficulty in Missouri, and that he therefore can not act in the matter as freely as he would desire.

Desiring only the good of the cause in which we are engaged, I know you will indulge me in a suggestion of a matter of importance in connexion with this subject. Col Spates is deservedly popular with the Administration at Washington. Any reasonable request he makes will be granted. In a conversation had with him this morning, I suggested that he raise a Regiment for the Potomac Home Brigade, and to my gratification the idea was responded to favorably. I do not know that he would attach himself permanently to it if it took him from his present engagement as President of the Canal Co. But, I believe if the Governor will suggest the matter to him he will do it, and if he does he will <u>settle the matter of Brig Gen just as certain as that the sun shines</u> and that too without any further trouble on the part of the true friends of the Brigade. This you may rely upon. Suggest it to our

*worthy Col. Maulsby and the Governor as soon as
possible. With his aid I believe we could get all or nearly
all the fugitives from Va. now scattered along the line of
Canal, together with others inapproachable by any other
source.*

*Gov. Thomas and Col. Maulsby, permit me to say,
have been kind to me. They are the first to offer me aid
since I was forced from my busness, in Greenbrier and
Allegany Counties, Virginia last December, and I feel the
more anxious, therefore to render all the aid I can to them
personally, and to you and our Common Cause, generally,
and I assure you that if Col. S. can be engaged as above
suggested and the whole matter left in his hands, Col.
Thruston will never be the Brig. Gen. of the Pot. Home
Brigade. I believe if he were appointed to-day that in less
than a fortnight Spates and every prominent officer on the
line would be under arrest- and I think Spates feard this-
hence he is interested in arresting this thing &c.*

I could say more were I with you

Truly Yours   D. Blocher

The Col. Spates, referred to above, is Alfred Spates
who became President of the Chesapeake and Potomac
Canal Company in 1861. It appears, from Mr. Blocher's
remarks, that a lobbying campaign was being waged to
have Mr. Spates appointed as Brigadier General to
command the Potomac Home Brigade. The appointment
never took place. Spates served throughout the War as the
Canal Company President and was recognized as having

performed a great service by keeping military supplies moving on the canal.

It is unclear to which "Mr. Blair" Blocher is referring. It would be either Montgomery Blair, the Post Master General or his brother Frank Blair, the United States Senator from Missouri. In any case, the "Fremont difficulty in Missouri" is undoubtedly a reference to General John C. Fremont, the commander of the army in the west. He occasioned monumental consternation in the government and on the part of Lincoln by unilaterally issuing a proclamation confiscating slaves and proclaiming their emancipation. This action occurred on August 30,1861, much before President Lincoln was ready, or indeed, was the country as a whole to contemplate the question of emancipation. Fremont's proclamation was promulgated without authority and led directly to his being removed from his position, and because of his immense popularity among the Abolitionists, was not cashiered, but relegated to the backwater of West Virginia. It was not long, however, that the backwater became a hot spot in the Valley Campaign.

Lincoln's primary concern was to prevent the border states of Missouri, Kentucky, and especially Maryland, from leaving the Union by prematurely turning the War into a conflict to liberate the slaves. Therefore, Fremont's jumping the gun, was antithetical to the President's strategic purpose.

In his capacity as head recruiter, Mr. Blocher wrote the following to Colonel Maulsby:

135

Balt. Sept 30th 61

Col W. P. Maulsby

     Dear Sir

        I have been requested to forward the two recruits sent today to your care for the "Maulsby Guard".

        I think we will be able to send daily more or less, until the Co. is filled.

Truly Yours

D. Blocher

Again, in his capacity as recruiter, Blocher penned the following to Colonel Maulsby:

Baltimore Nov 8th 61

Col. W. P. Maulsby,

     Dear Sir

        I herewith send you in charge of Mr. W. A. Scarborough, 6 men for the Maulsby Guard, to be under the command of Capt. Scarborough, as suggested in my note of yesterday. If you will send the bearer of this (Scarborough) back for a few days he will be of service in recruiting here. I owe some twenty Dollars for Rents, Adv. &c which, if Col. Dennis will send me I will account for on my arrival at Fred'k.

Truly Yours D. Blocher

Mr. Scarborough's name is not to be found in any of the Potomac Home Brigade Rosters, so it appears that the proposed appointment never occurred.

Regimental Quartermaster Blocher wrote to Colonel Maulsby regarding two horses. The original of this document belongs to the author.

136

Camp Worman, Jan. 3d 1862

Wm P. Maulsby, Col. Com. 1st Regt. Home Brigade, vol.

Sir:

I find, upon examination, two horses in the employ of the Quartermasters Department, in the 1st Md. Regt. Pot. H. Brigade Vols. unfit for use. Therefore as per direction of Revised Army Regulations, pages 153, paragraph 1025, I respectfully call the attention of the Commanding officer to the fact, in order that they may be disposed of according to Rule.

Respectfully Yours
D. Blocher AQM
1st Md. Reg. P.H.B.

The Maulsby Papers contains this next letter.

Clearspring Sep 21/61

Col Maulsby

Sir

Yours of the 19th has been recd. We fully appreciate the course you have marked out for yourself and commend you for it. It only remains for us to say that Mr. Mathews belongs to the second class you name, he has a son in law and a nephew in Capt. Prather's Camp. and has been, and still is doing all he can, to promote the interests of the glorious cause you and us have so much at heart. as Mr. M. will be the bearer of this, we need say not more. You will do right, we have no doubt.

Yours Respty.
C. Kalbjus

The following letter was sent to Regimental Headquarters in Frederick.

Liberty Town Oct. 4th 1861

To Genl E. Shriner & Col. G. R. Dennis

Gent

The bearer Mr. Willson who will hand you this wishes to have your aid in getting his son who has left him for the purpose of enlisting Any aid you can give him will be thankfully received by him his son is not 18 years of Age and you can rely upon any statement Mr. Willson will make in regard to the matter. I shall be pleased if you will aid him in getting his son.

Yours Truly

Francis S. Jones

Another very interesting letter in the same vein reads as follows:

Baltimore Oct. 9th 1861

To Colonel Wm P. Maulsby

Dear Sir

The undersigned citizens of Baltimore have learned that their sons Thomas G. Murdock and John Henry Piercy, have enlisted in the Service of the 1st Regiment Pot. Home Brigade, under your command. Whilst we appreciate the object of the formation of your Regiment, and are willing to do all in our power to promote the interests of our Country in her present struggle against internal enemies, we cannot agree

*that boys so young and consequently incompetent should
be exposed to the hardships of war and to the utter
destruction of their phisical constitution- neither of them
being yet <u>sixteen years of age.</u> We therefore beg that you
will send them home, without trouble to us, as times are
hard and we have been informed by Mr. Blocher that you
will do us justice in the matter without the necessity of our
coming up or swering out a writ of <u>Habeas Corpus.</u>*

*We hope Sir you will have an interview with the
boys, and let us hear from you on the subject as early as
possible.*

John Murdock
Jacob H. Piercy

Please direct to
John Murdock No 39 Stile St. Balt.

Another letter on the general theme of running away
from home to join the Army was sent to Colonel Maulsby
from Baltimore. It reads:

Baltimore Oct 9th 1861

Col. William P. Maulsby

Dear Sir

*At the instance of a distressed family I
address this note to you. The Father William Allen left his
home on last Wednesday under a state of Excitement
which has caused the most painful anxiety upon the part of
his wife and children as to his probable course.*

*From Enquiries his wife is induced to believe he has
gone to Frederick for the purpose of Enlisting in one of*

the Regiments in the vicinity of that City and probably the
one under your command. He is an Englishman by birth
but has been in this country for some years. About 5 feet
8 in Hight thick set, with broad forehead Brown hair and
grey on the Eyes speaks very broad rather more of the
Scotch that English dialect, about Fifty two or three years
of age and a weaver by trade he has left a wife and five
children. If any person answering the discription is to be
found amongst the military please do an act of
philanthropy by writing me as soon as possible and relieve
a distressed family.

Very Respectfully
Benjn Haughey

Please direct me in the
care of Edwd Peters Esqr
corner of St. Paul & Lexington St.

Dr. William A. Martin of Uniontown in Carroll
County, Maryland sent Lieutenant-Colonel Dennis the
following two letters:

Union Town
Nov. 8th 1861

Geo. R. Dennis

Leut. Col. 1st Maryland Regt.
Potomac Home Brigade

I hereby certify that Mr. Alfred Shriner of your command
applied to me for medical treatment he is suffering from
Rheumatism contracted in camp. he is not fit for duty. I

would advise a lengthening of his furlough for 8 or 10 days.

> *Yours Resp.*
> *Wm. A. Martin*
> *Practicing Physician*
> *Union Town*
> *Md.*

His furlough expires on Tuesday the 12 Inst.

> *Union Town*
> *Nov. 15th 1861*

To Geo. R. Dennis, Lieut. Col.
> *1st Maryland Regmt.*
> *Potomac Home Brigade*

I hereby certify that Alfred Shriner Esq. of your command has been under my professional care since his return from camp. he is suffering from subacute Rheumatism-contracted before leaving camp-

he is unable to perform camp duty or to bear the exposure of camp. I advise you to give him an extension of furlough until well.

> *Yours Resp.*
> *Wm. A. Martin*
> *Practicing Physician*

Note: Alfred Shriner was a Private in Company G, First Regiment.

Dr. J. J. Weaver, also of Uniontown, wrote on behalf of another sick soldier:

Union Town Md Nov. 8th 61
To Geo. R. Dennis Lt. Co. First Md.
Regt. Pot. home Brgad.

> *Dear Sir I have been called to see David Bloom of Capt. Yallots Company and find him labouring under symptoms of Pleuria Pneumonia with some effusion of the left side. He is not able to be out of his room, much less to be on camp duty, and will not be able to go under ten days or two weeks. Please send him a furlough for that time.*

Yours Resply.
J. J. Weaver
Practicing Physician of Uniontown
Carroll Co. Md.

Note: Private Bloom apparently recovered, because he served for three years.

Another request for a furlough extension was sent to Colonel Maulsby, but this time, not from a doctor. It reads:

Head Quarters 12 Regt Ind. Vol.
Camp near Sharpsburg Md
Nov 17, 1861

Col Wm. P. Malsby

> *Sir Wm. Sharer a private in Capt. Cronise Co. of your Regt. is here on furlough which expires he says tomorrow.*

142

I have to request that you will if not inconsistant with the good of the service extend his furlough some ten days. We have it in contemplation to cross, providing anything turns out as we desire before long & as he has lost considerable property he wishes to be along with us to try to secure some of his own- he could also be of much benefit to me in the event of our crossing.

Yours Truly

M. H. Link Col

12 R. I. V.

Comdg.

William Sharer is listed on the roster of Company H, First Regiment, which was the second company of Sharpsburg Rifles along with R. E. Cook's Company A.

In late November, 1861, Lieutenant-Colonel Dennis received a letter of complaint from Jeremiah Cramer. It reads:

Nover 24, 1861

Harmony Grove Fredk Co Md

Col Dennis

Dear Sir

The teams are still Hauling wood. I am exceedingly sorry that you told the Quarter Master about it I am apprehensive that He will Keep on Sending the teams until their wont be a Stick left me for winter.

I am fearful that you will be the means of losing Considerable on that wood. I could have gotten three and a Quarter for Every cord of that wood but Nevertheless I Charge two and Half for it So if the Quarter Master

Does not allow me that I Hope you will make up the
deficiency as you were the means of getting it away.

 I hope you will not get affronted at what I Have
written to you for It was not intended for that purpose.

Yours &c

Jeremiah C. Cramer

 The next document is in the collection of Potomac
Home Brigade documents at the Frederick County
Historical Society.

Headquarters Gen. Banks' Division

Frederick City, Md.

Dec. 5th 1861

Special Orders
 No. 398

VI.......<u>Assignment of "Home Guard" of Maryland.</u>

Headquarters, Army of the Potomac

Washington, Nov. 28th 1861

Special Orders

   No. 161

    16._ The Division of Major Gen'l.
Banks, will take up a position at or in the vicinity of
Frederick City, to be selected by the Division
Commander, who is also assigned to the Command
of the Maryland Home guards raised in that
quarter.   *By Command of*
Major Gen'l. McClellan

    (Signed). S. Williams, Asst. Adjt.
Gen'l.

Officers Commanding regiments and Detachments of

Home Guards, will report to Major Gen'l. Banks, for duty
immediately.

X   X   X   X   X   X   X   X

> *By Command of*
> *Major Gen'l. Banks*
> *R. Morris Copeland*
> *Asst. Adjt. Gen'l.*

To

> *Colonel Maulsby*
> *1st Regt. Maryland "Home Brigade".*

As noted previously, the Fourth Regiment was only
partially formed and was later merged with the Third. The
following "Special Orders" is in the Frederick County
Historical Society's files:

> *Head Quarters, Gen'l. Banks'*
Division

> *Frederick City, Md.*
> *Dec. 16th 1861*

Special orders
  No 407

x   x   x   x   x   x   x   x

X........... Lieut. Col. G. R. Dennis, 1st Rt. Maryland
"Home Brigade", is hereby detailed at the request of
Governor Thomas to take charge of the 4th Regt. "Home
Brigade", now recruiting at Williamsport.

x   x   x   x   x   x   x   x

> *By Command of*

Major Gen'l. Banks
Asst. Adj't. Gen'l.

To

Col. Maulsby
Comm. of 1st Md "Home Brigade"

A very interesting document related to the daily existence of the troops is the following order from Division Headquarters which is indicative of the bureaucratic proclivities common to the military, even to the present day. The original is in the author's collection.

Head Quarters Gen'l. Banks' Division
Frederick City, Md. Jan. 3d 1862

General Orders
    No. 19}

    On and after this date, all mounted messengers found riding their horses faster than the exigency of the Order demands, shall be punished for violating "General Orders", relating thereto. Henceforth, all Orders and Dispatches, will be marked on the wrapper, the pace at which they are to be carried; and any deviation from the Order will be severely punished.

By Command of
Major General Banks
R. Morris Copeland
Asst. Adj't. General

Col. W.P. Maulsby
1st Maryland "Home Brigade"

_____XXX_____

At the end of 1861, the newly appointed Chaplain of the First Regiment, William G. Ferguson, submitted his quarterly report. The original of this document is housed at the Historical Society of Frederick County.

Col Wm P Maulsby: Col commanding First Regt Potomac Home Brigade, Maryland Volunteers.

        Dear Sir: in accordance with the 9th sec of "an act to authorize the employment of volunteers to aid in enforcing the laws; and protecting public property, approved July 22nd 1861, I hereby present to you my quarterly report for the quarter ending December 31st 1861.

        The moral condition of the Regt. (while it is not all could be desired) I am glad to say is quite flattering. It has been my pleasure during the last six months to move among many of the Regts. that have been, and still are, in the service of the United States of America; and I am glad to say that I have heard less profanity, and seen less drunkenness in the Maryland First Potomac Home Brigade, than in any other; whether this is the result of the fear of God, on the part the various members of the Regt. I am sorry I can not say so much. I fear that a lack of steadfastness, peculiarity of surroundings, deprivation for three or four months from the ordinary means of grace without any one to care for their souls, or something else has been the cause (on the part of a few at least) of a lukewarmness which is always dangerous, but I am glad to say that a number seem to be alarmed at their condition, and hope through the grace of God to make improvement in the future.

During the quarter I have been enabled through the kindness of the "Young Men's bible society of Frederick County" to place in the hands of every member of the Regt. a copy of the New Testament Scriptures, which have been generaly gladly received, and in many instances, I know, read with pleasure, and I trust, with profit.

I have just now no suggestions to make such as may conduce to the social happiness and moral improvement of the troops, save one. I have noticed both at the Hospital, and in camp, that certain species of work is done on the Lord's day which a raw recruit like myself would be apt to think might as well be done at some other time, and during divine service I have several time heard the strokes of the axe. There are other things which possibly it would have been proper to have noticed in this Report, but as I have been in the service but two weeks I leave them for the future.

All of which is respectfully submitted.
Wm. G Ferguson Chaplain
1st Regt Potomac Home Brigade
Maryland Volunteers

Chaplain Ferguson submitted his next quarterly report on March 31, 1862. The original is in the author's collection and is quoted below.

Colonel William P. Maulsby, Col. Commanding 1st Maryland Regt Potomac Home Brigade Volunteers

Honored Sir: in accordance with an act of Congress approved July 22nd 1861 I herewith present to you my Quarterly Report for the Quarter ending March 31st 1862.

Since my last Report (Dec 31st 1861) we have been two months in Winter Quarters almost the whole of which time was spent (as far as the vast majority of the Regt was concerned) in idleness. The weather was bad, with almost continual rain, making our Camp in such a condition, that Company and Regimental drill were for weeks together utterly impossible. Idleness is not only subversive of good order, but also of good morals; and as this is admitted in Town and Country, it is but natural to suppose it to be a most potent power for evil in a Military Camp. In addition to this, on account of bad weather our Sunday services were frequently interrupted; and at times the way of usefulness seemed almost closed up. Having for many years held service twice every Sabbath without any interruption, this was to me a cause of much affliction, but when I remember that the weather was all controlled by a far seeing Providence, I derived pleasure from knowing that I stood at my Post ready to work as opportunity offered. In order to be more useful, I left my quarters in Mr. Worman's House, on the 25th January, and moved inside the lines of the Camp, shoveling away the snow, and raising my tent in which I lived until the Regt left for Virginia Feb. 26th. While at Camp Worman in order to be more useful, I formed a Bible Class, and established a Library, which has furnished reading matter for all who chose to avail themselves of it; whether officers, or men:

149

in addition to this I found, and distributed, many copies of Dr Hall's little pamphlet called "Take Care of Your Health", besides hundreds of copies of the "Christian Banner for the Soldier and the Sailor", and thousands of pages of Tracts. During the prevalence of the measles among us, I found an open field of labor among the sick, and dying in the Hospital which I visited every day.

I am glad to say that during the Quarter several have found peace in believing; and if the testimony and correct walk of a soldier indicates anything, I have no reason to doubt the reality of their conversion, while I have hope in the death of a number who died during the winter. Of the brave lads who were snatched from us by the ruthless hand of death, I attended all their burials save a few who were taken away to their friends, and one who was buried near our Camp without my knowledge. I have no "suggestions to make such as may conduce to the social happiness and moral improvement of the troops", nor any further report.

Your Obedient Servant

W. G. Ferguson Chaplain

1st Md Regt Potomac Home

Brigade

Carter House Charlestown

March 31st 1862

The History and Roster of Maryland Volunteers states that Chaplain Ferguson resigned from the service on February 28, 1862. This, by virtue of the above-quoted report, must be in error, since he was in the company of the Regiment in Charlestown on March 31.

The collection of Potomac Home Brigade documents in the library of the Historical Society of Frederick county contains this commendation from the War Department dated Sept. 7, 1862:

Captain William Yontz, Company E, Potomac Home Brigade detached at Edmond's Ferry on the Potomac was attacked on Sept. 4, 1862 thus "spilling the first Rebel blood on Maryland soil."

In addition to the four regiments of infantry originally authorized by Secretary Cameron, Francis Thomas was granted authority to raise four companies of cavalry. The official letter of authorization reads as follows:

War Department,
Washington, July 26, 1861
Hon. Francis Thomas, Frederick, Md.:

Sir, The four companies of cavalry offered by you, one to be attached to each of the four regiments of infantry, heretofore accepted, are accepted for three years or the war.

This acceptance is with the distinct understanding that the Department will revoke the commissions of all officers who may be found incompetent for the proper discharge of their duties.

You will advise Adjt. Gen. Thomas, at Washington, the date at which the men will be ready for mustering, and he will detail an officer for that purpose.

By order of the Secretary of War.
James Lesley, Jr., Chief Clerk

Recruiting for the cavalry companies began as soon as the above authorization was received. These companies were organized as independent entities at first. The battalion was given the informal title of "Cole's Cavalry." The official muster of Company A took place on August 8, 1861, with Senior Captain Henry A. Cole in command. The First Lieutenant was Richard W. Coomes and Second Lieutenant was George W. F. Vernon.

Company B was commanded by Captain William Fiery with Alexander M. Flory as First Lieutenant and Jacob A. Metz, as Second Lieutenant.

Company C was recruited at Gettysburg in August, 1861 and was officially mustered in at Frederick on August 27, 1861. John Horner was Captain; John M. Annan, First Lieutenant; and Washington Morrison, Second Lieutenant.

D Company was commanded by Captain Pearce K. Curll with Robert H. Milling, First Lieutenant and Francis Gallagher, Second Lieutenant.

The four companies were consolidated into the First Regiment Potomac Home Brigade Cavalry in June, 1862 under the Command of Henry A. Cole who was promoted to the rank of Major on August 1st of that year. Until the spring of 1864, the four companies operated as a battalion, when it was increased to full regiment status by the addition of eight companies. At this time Cole was promoted to Colonel. "Cole's Cavalry" served with distinction and was involved in numerous skirmishes and actions from October, 1861, to September, 1864. It captured in excess of one thousand prisoners, and captured or destroyed huge quantities of Confederate stores, ordinance, and equipment. The regiment was mustered out on June 28, 1865.

During the Centennial years of the Civil War, 1959 to 1965, The Potomac Edison Company published a monthly newspaper named the <u>Valley News Echo</u>. Each issue contains contemporary articles from newspapers in communities in the Shenandoah and Potomac River Valleys during the War. All items quoted are by permission of the Potomac Edison Company.

The Centennial newspaper of August, 1961 contains the following notice:

Maulsby Named Colonel
of First Regiment, PHB

TRAIL, FIERY APPOINTED

Frederick, MD., August 17 - William P. Maulsby, of this city, has been appointed by the President of the United States as Colonel of the newly Formed First Regiment of the Potomac Home Brigade.

On July 19, ex-Governor Francis Thomas received authorization from Simon Cameron, U.S. Secretary of War, to "provide for the organization of four regiments of loyal citizens resident on both sides of the Potomac River from the Monocacy to the western boundary of Maryland, for the protection of the canal and of the property and persons of loyal citizens of the neighborhood, and to be stationed in the vicinity whilst in the service."

Thomas, who is a member of the U. S. House of Representatives, organized four companies of cavalry, composed of citizens from this area. On July 26, the Federal government accepted these companies for three years service and assigned one company to each of the four regiments of infantry. The entire force has been designated as the Potomac Home Brigade.

Other officers appointed to lead the First Regiment of the Potomac Home Brigade are: Charles E. Trail of Frederick County, lieutenant colonel; and Lewis P. Fiery of Washington County, major.

Seven companies have already been mustered into service. They have encamped near the turnpike, about a mile and a half north of this city. Eight companies have been raised in Allegany County.

As an inducement for enlisting in the Brigade, an offer of $13 per month for clothing and a bounty of $100 is offered each enlistee. A tract of "bounty land" is also promised every soldier who enlists.

An additional item of interest from the same issue reads thus:

Thomas Johns Appointed
Colonel, 2nd Regiment

Officers named

Cumberland, MD., August 21 - The Second Regiment of Infantry of the Potomac Home Brigade was organized here with Thomas Johns, of this city, as colonel.

The other field officers of the regiment are: Robert Bruce of this city, lieutenant colonel; J. Ellis Porter, of Lonaconing, major; Orlando D. Robbins, adjutant; Kennedy H. Butler, quartermaster; Samuel P. Smith, surgeon; and John H. Symmes, chaplain.

The following companies and their commanders have been organized: Company A, Capt. Alexander Shaw, at Lonaconing; Company B, Capt. James D. Roberts, at Old Town; Company C, Capt. John H. Huntley, at Frostburg; Company D, Capt. Benjamin B. Shaw, at Piedmont, Va.; Company E, Capt. James C. Lynn, at Cumberland; Company F, Capt. Lewis Dyche, at Hancock; Company G, Capt. Charles G. McClelland, at Mount Savage; Company H, Capt. George H. Bragonier, at Cumberland; Company I, Capt. J. Floyd McCulloch, at Allegany County at large; and Company K, Capt. Peter B. Petrie, at Cumberland.

The August edition of the <u>Valley News Echo</u> also contains the following very interesting item from the papers of August, 1861.

Attempt to Wreck Train
Made Near Cumberland

Ex-Governor Aboard

Cumberland, MD., August 24 - An attempt was made today to wreck the train, ten miles west of this city, on which ex-Governor of Maryland Francis Thomas was traveling.

Thomas addressed a meeting of citizens of this city yesterday evening on the subject of forming a regiment for the Potomac Home Brigade. During the talk, he was interrupted by a man making accusations against the Federal Government. The crowd attacked the man, who was defended by the editor of the _Democratic Alleganian_. The crowd then went to the office of the _Alleganian_ and wrecked the building. They then went to the residence of Senator Thomas J. McKaig, where they broke several windows.

Thomas has given the following account of today's incident:

"I left here (Cumberland) this morning at half past six for my home, on the railroad train. Ten miles from this place the cow catcher of the engine ran against a pile of eight railroad ties, which had been carefully placed across the track. Fortunately six of the ties were scattered right and left of the road, and the train continued to run for about 500 yards when it was stopped by the resistance to its progress produced by the two remaining ties, which were so situated that one end rested on the engine and the other plowed along the road.

"As soon as the cars halted the engineer and fireman leaped off and soon removed the two ties, while the baggage master was out to see what had occurred to arrest our progress. All this happened in almost an instant, and before I had paid much attention to what was occurring. At that moment the baggage master exclaimed, 'there is an armed man on the road behind us!' This caused the thought to flash across my mind that this *accident had been contrived, and I called the conductor to the platform on which I stood and directed him to put the cars in motion by pulling the bell-rope. The conductor seemed at a loss to know how to act, but obeyed my directions, and as soon as the train began to move, we were fired upon by a crowd of more than one hundred armed men who had appeared upon the road out of the bushes near the spot where the ties had been placed on the road.*

"We all escaped uninjured, although twenty or thirty shots were fired before we were out of reach. There were no persons on the train as passengers but two aged men and myself. This whole nefarious affair was, I have no doubt, contrived against my liberty, if not my life, by spies resident in this place who notified their allies in Virginia that I was to pass on the railroad this morning. And nothing saved me but that coolness and presence of mind, which prompted me, under Providence, to see and guard against the danger prompt as electricity."

The Diary Of Jacob Engelbrecht, published by The Historical Society of Frederick County, and edited by William Quynn, contains a number of references to the Potomac Home Brigade during the period of time encompassed by this book. Englebrecht, born in Frederick in 1797, was the son of Conrad Englebrecht who came from Germany as one of the Hessian Mercenaries hired by the British in the Revolutionary War. After being captured and held at the "Hessian Barracks" in Frederick, Conrad elected to stay and become an American. Jacob was

trained to follow in his father's trade as a tailor. He kept a
diary of the daily comings and goings and notable events in
Frederick beginning in 1819 and continued for sixty years.
During the Civil War, Jacob was a storekeeper on West
Patrick Street, the main east-west thoroughfare through the
town. This provided him with a front-row seat from which
to view many of the significant events which occurred in
Frederick in the course of the War. Shortly after the War
Mr. Englebrecht served one term as Mayor of Frederick.

The quotations from the Englebrecht Diary are cited
with the permission of the Historical Society of Frederick
County, Inc. The first entries of note follow:

*"Cole Rangers" A Calvary Company raised by Henry A.
Cole in our town & vicinity mustered into the U. S. service
by Major Smith of U. S. Army Augt 10 1861 is the 1st
Company of Calvary 1st Regt of the Home Brigade of
Maryland. viz captain Henry A. Cole, ...* (He goes on to
name the entire Company) - *Total 85 rank & file
Wednesday August 14. 1861. - 8 ock a m*

*A Company of Soldiers Just now arrived in town from
Sharpsburg Washington County Md to attach themselves
to the Regt Maryland Volunteers at our Barracks - they
Number 100 & Commanded by Captn Cook
Thursday Augt 15. 1861. 11. ock a.m.*

*Command- in our town the Men (Soldiers) have nearly
all left. they (the 4th Connecticutt Regt) left on monday
evening (19th) & are encamped at the White Oak Springs*

a few miles South west of town - on tuesday last 20 inst a
company of 80 men under Captn Gidion Prather Came
here from Clear Spring, Washington Co. & were
Examined, inspected & enrolled in Maryland Regt U. S.
under Genl Cooper & yesterday, another Company, of 104
under Captn William Fiery arrived here from the Same
County. & are now being Examined at the City Hall by Dr
Jacob Baer.- to be Sworn in & enrolled, in the Same Regt.
Saturday Augt. 24. 1861. - 10. ock. a m

12th of september - to day being the anniversary of the
Battle of North Point & Bombardment of Fort McHenry
(in 1814) our Military are now Parading the streets of
our town - the "Home Guards" appear to day (for the first
time) in their uniform - there was a Flag. (Cost 35$)
presented to Captn Glessners Company at the Barracks
Hill this forenoon - there are 4.

Frederick Zouares. - which was Mustered in the 1st Regt
of Home Brigade Septr 18 1861 are as follows. Captain
Chas L. Baugher.... (He goes on to list the entire
Company)
Copied from the "Examiner" of today total 79
Wednesday Octr 2d 1861 2 ock pm

Troop of Horse. this morning at 6. o clock the Troop of
Horse numbering about 100. Captn Wm Fiery left our
Barrack for Williamsport & the upper Potomack they were
in our City about one month. they were nearly all from
Washington County. Maryland & Came here to be

159

mustered into Service. Get uniforms. Horses &c (Mr
Isaiah Loy is among them)
Saturday Octr 5 1861 - 11. ock a m

The Valley News Echo, October edition, printed a
notice related to the above entry.

Cavalry Arrives
At Cumberland

Cumberland, MD., Oct. 12 - The cavalry company
commanded by William Fiery attached to the Potomac
Home Brigade arrived here today from Frederick.

This regiment was raised principally at Clear
Spring in Washington County and will constitute a portion
of the Second Regiment of the Potomac Home Brigade,
the Allegany Regiment, which is located here. Each man
is armed with a Sharp's rifle and a navy revolver, and will
be furnished with a saber.

Fiery is a brother of Lewis P. Fiery of Washington
County, who is a Union candidate for State Senator.
Alexander Flory is first lieutenant of the company and
Albert Metz is second lieutenant.

Jacob Englelbrecht's diary continues with the next
entries which mention the Brigade.

John A. Steiner Esqr was Commissioned a Major in the 1st
Regt Potomack Home Brigade - he was qualified
according to Law. yesterday evening.
Wednesday Octr 23rd 1861. - 4. o'ck pm

160

Whiskey War, - a while ago a Detatchment of the Home
Brigade. at the Barracks made a sortie on Several of the
"Grog-Shops" in town and destroyed two Barrels of
Whiskey & Several Demijohns of liquor - for John Bates,
east end of Second street (Sherbro) & also Six Barrels of
Whiskey & other Liquors for Wm H. Borcher in east
Church Street (Wm Adams house) & I believe are Still on
the Scout for more, - they have often forbidden (the
Commanders of the Brigade) from Selling Liquor to the
Soldiers - but they would do it -. and this is the
consequence -
Tuesday Octr 29. 1861 11 ock a m

Research at the Maryland Historical Society in
Baltimore has yielded some very interesting information
found in their newspaper archives. The <u>Frederick
Examiner</u> of July 31, 1861 printed the following:

NOTICE

ATTENTION

FREDERICK HOME GUARDS

You are hereby ordered to meet at your armory, ON
THIS WEDNESDAY EVENING, July 31st. Every member
should be in attendence as business importance is to be
transacted.

by order,

David T. Bennett, Captain

On August 28, 1861 <u>The Republican</u> printed this
dispatch.

AFFAIRS IN FREDERICK COUNTY

[From the Frederick Examiner, Aug. 28]

Seizure of Arms.- About two o'clock on last Thursday morning a company of Indiana volunteers from Gen. Banks' column, called at the house of Mr. N. Stevens in New Market, and demanded the surrender of a quantity of arms, supposed to be secreted on the premises. After some parley, Mr. Stevens brought down from the second story some twenty odd U. S. rifles which had been secreted between the floor and ceiling. The Indianians obtained several more from other places, making in all twenty-nine. We also hear, that these guns have been placed by Gen. Banks' order in the hands of Captain Cole's cavalry of Home Brigade, for guard service in camp, until their own arms shall be furnished.

New Military Telegraph.- We learn that a telegraphic line now connects Major Gen. Banks Head-quarters near Hyattstown, twelve miles S. E. of this city on the Georgetown road, with the War Department at Washington. The erection of this line will give great expedition to any contemplated movement of the troop in Gen. Banks' division.

The October 16, 1861 edition of <u>The Republican</u> contained these dispatches from Frederick.

AFFAIRS IN FREDERICK

(From the Examiner, Oct. 16.)

Death of Captain Prather.- The melancholy duty devolves upon us of announcing the untimely death of

162

Captain S. Gideon Prather, Captain of the "Clearspring Infantry", of the first regiment Maryland Home Guard. This event transpired at two o'clock yesterday morning, at the residence of Hiram Winchester, Esq., in the Frederick Female Seminary. His disease was inflamation of the brain, resulting from billious intermittent fever. His age was 29 years.

Death of a Venerable Citizen.- On Saturday last, at his residence one mile and a half north of this city, Moses Worman, a much respected citizen, departed this life, in the fullness of years, and with an unsullied reputation for integrity and benevolence. Mr Worman was 84 years, 9 months and 7 days old, at the time of his death, and in all the vicissitudes of this long and eventful period was an active, useful and upright citizen, a sincere friend, and a man of fixed principles. For many years, while the patriotism of the old Whig party breasted the fury of its opponents with undaunted front and confident reliance in the integrity of its purposes, Mr Worman was the constant Chairman of the County Central Committee, and his name was of itself a sufficient voucher for the purity of the party whose banner he upheld. He acquired, by a career of honest thrift as an agriculturalist, a handsome fortune. His remains were interred at Mount Olivet Cemetery on Sunday afternoon, attended by a numerous concourse of mourning relatives and friends.

Removal of Camps.- The first regiment of the Home Brigade removed their camp on Monday last from the Barracks field to the rear of the farm of Lieutenant

163

Colonel G. R. Dennis, about two miles north of this city,
where a very fine camp ground has been selected and
occupied. One reason for the removal, we hear, was
consideration for the sick in Hospital at the Barracks, who
are thus relieved from the noise and bustle attendant upon
a regiment.

Based on the above, it is not a stretch of the
imagination to speculate on the origin of the naming the
First Regiment's bivouac as Camp Worman.

<u>The Diary of Jacob Engelbrecht</u> contains several
references to Camp Worman and are worth noting here.
The 1st Regt Maryland Potomack Home Brigade under
Col. Wm P. Maulsby passed the Shop door Just now, on
their way to Wormans field to encamp there- they had been
at the Barracks for several Months- the Barracks field will
be occupied by a part of Genl Banks's Column from
Darnestown.
Wednesday Decr 4. 1861. 1 1/2 ock pm

Review. Major Genl Banks. had a review to day of 5 Regt
at Wormans Field. on the Monococy. near the Toll-gate, viz
3d Wisconsin Regt 29th Pennsylvania- 9th New York & 27
Indianna- our first Regt of Potomack Home Brigade were
present. as Spectators but not reviewed. We have now in &
near of City about 15 regiments about 15,000 men
Thursday decr 12th 1861.- 4. ock pm

And another Review- to day (afternoon) General
Abercrombies Regt (or rather several Regiments) will be

reviewed by Genl Banks. at Potts' farm Down the Turnpike
(2 miles nearly) Moving of troops- Last night about 8 o'ck
two Cavalry companies Captns Horner & Cole. left for the
upper Potomack, and at 10. oclock 3 Batteries (Brass
Cannon) passed, also westward, and at 11. ock the 29th
Regt Pa volunteers passed through Patrick Street- this Regt
was encamped on the land of Mr Francis Markell over
Monococy (Gibralter farm) - I suppose there will be a
little Rumpus in Virginia
Thursday Dec 19 1861 8 ock a m

Yesterday afternoon I went to the Michigan Encampment
beyond Wormans- on the Creagerstown Road in Wormans
Woods- opposite the Harmony Grove school-house- the
Maryland Regt Col. Maulsby is on the left hand Side
opposite the "Michiganders"-
Monday Decr 23. 1861. - 8 1/2 am

Although not specifically related to the subject of
this book, this entry from Engelbrecht's Diary should be of
general interest to the reader.

95 years - this day Mrs Barbara Fritchie. widow of the late
John Casper Fritchie, is 95 years old - she was born "Decr
3 1766" She lives opposite our residence at the Bentz
Bridge - is very active for a person of her age.

The <u>Valley News Echo</u> for November cites the
following:

Colorful Flag Given
To "Allegany Regiment"

Presented by Shriver

Receipt Acknowledged

Cumberland, Md., Nov.9- A handsome regimental flag was presented to the Second Regiment of the Potomac Home Brigade, The "Allegany Regiment", commanded by Col. Thomas Johns, by Robert Shriver of this city.

The regiment was unexpectedly called away from this city thereby preventing a public presentation of the flag. The flag is of blue silk with heavy bullion fringe. On one side is the national coat of arms; on the other side, the title "Second Regiment Potomac Home Brigade" is emblazoned.

The regiment is now stationed at Camp Thomas (named for Francis Thomas)? *near Romney, Va. Johns sent the following letter to Shriver today acknowledging the flag:*

"In the name of the Second Regiment, Potomac Home Brigade, I have the honor to thank you for the handsome regimental flag presented by you to this regiment. We accept it as a token of your high appreciation of our loyalty and patriotism, and will endeavor bravely to bear it aloft until this the land." sic

President Lincoln issued an executive order on November 27, 1861, designating Thursday, November 28,

1861, as a Day of Thanksgiving and announcing the closure of all government departments. The text of the order reads:

Executive Mansion. Washington, 27th. November, 1861.

The Municipal authorities of Washington and Georgetown in this District, have appointed tomorrow, the 28th, instant, as a day of thanksgiving, the several Departments will on that occasion be closed, in order that the officers of the government may partake in the ceremonies.   *Abraham Lincoln*

This action helped established the tradition of the official national holiday we now call Thanksgiving Day. The November 27, 1861, issue of the <u>Frederick Examiner</u> contains an item related to the Holiday and reads:

MILITARY BALL- A grand military ball will be given at Junior Hall to-morrow evening by the First Regiment of the Potomac Home Brigade to celebrate Thanksgiving Day. Extensive preparations have been made to give the affair eclat, and to preserve puntilions (sic) order; and it promises to be a brilliant and well conducted ball.- Good music and a set supper are among the attractions, and the beauty of the city is expected to lend its charms to the gay and festive scene. The committee of arrangements consists of Captains Cole, Glessner, and Yontz and Lieuts. Whittier and Bamford, - names that are an ample guaranty for good order and enjoyment.

The above-mentioned Junior Hall was on the second floor of the Junior Fire Company No. 2 situated next door to the Farmers & Mechanics Bank on the southeast corner of North Market and Second Streets. The name was derived from the original one of the Young Mens Fire Co. and also the name given to a new engine acquired in 1839, called Junior, because of the youth of the members.

A militia company was formed by the members and named the Junior Defenders. Their leader was Captain William Glessner, and on Friday, September 6, 1861, they were mustered in as Company B, First Regiment, Potomac Home Brigade. Jacob Engelbrecht recorded the event in his diary thus:

Captn Wm Glessners Company. were to day Mustered into the U. States Service, by Major Smith U. S. A.   Joseph Groff 1st Lieut. - G. T. Castle 2d Lieut, Friday Septr 6. 1861 - 9. ock a m

The Frederick Examiner edition of December 4, 1861, reported:

POTOMAC HOME BRIGADE.- Lt. Col. G. R. Dennis late of the 1st Regiment Potomac Home Brigade, has been appointed Lt. Col. of the Fourth Regiment now forming. The First Regiment being filled, Col Wm. P. Maulsby has assumed command and appointed Wm. Maulsby, Jr. Adjutant. Thomas Wolfe, Quartermaster of the same Regiment, has resigned as such.

GEN. BANKS' DIVISION.- Our city has been filled with rumors for some days past, of the removal to this vicinity of Maj. Gen. Banks' Division of the Army of the Potomac, and yesterday morning, tidings came that the 3rd Wisconsin Regiment, attached to the second brigade under Gen Hamilton, had reached Bennett's Creek, 8 miles South of this city, on its way hither. The almost impassable condition of the roads in Montgomery County and the exhaustion of forage are given as reasons for the removal; while some say the army is going into Winter quarters near this city, and others regard the change as preparatory to an advance movement into Virginia. As we know nothing of the plans of Maj. Gen. Banks, we leave the reader to his own conclusions; but we certainly do not think it is his intention to put his army in Winter quarters in Maryland.

P. S.- At 4 O'clock yesterday afternoon, Maj. Gen. N. P. Banks, accompanied by his staff, and body guard of the Van Allen Cavalry, arrived at this city, and was escorted to his quarters in W. Second St. by the First Reg't. Potomac Home Brigade. Gen. Banks' staff consists of Major R. Morris Copeland, Asst. Adj. Gen.; Capt. D. D. Perkins, 4th Artillery, Inspector; and Chief of Staff; Aides de Camp: Capt. R. S. Schriber, Capt. Schiffler and Mr. D'Haudeville; Quartermaster- Capts. Hollibird and Bingham, U. S. A.; Commissary, Capt. Beckwith, U. S. A.; Medical Director, Surgeon Wm. S. King, U. S. A.

__THE FREDERICK EXAMINER__ of December 11,1861, published the following:

LOCAL

Gen. Banks' Division.- Our usual quiet inland city is now all life and bustle; business is brisk, throngs of soldiers and citizens crowd the streets incessantly, while the passing to and fro of detachments of troops, enlivened with the notes of the drum and fife, the inspiriting bugle and music from military bands, the brilliant and varied military costumes and the rush of ladies attracted by the gardens and tempted forth by the balmy atmosphere, conspire to give a strange and exciting aspect to the town, and it is difficult in the din and apparent confusion to recognize its identity. Nor does the staid denizen feel a whit more at home when he traverses the limits of the corporation; the old familiar land marks are there, but camps encounter him on every road. A short drive on the Northern turnpike lands him in the midst of the First Regiment of the Potomac Home Brigade; on the east, the fields are whitened with the teeming tents of Gen. Hamilton's Second Brigade of Gen. Banks' Division; a little lower down, the sides of the railroad near Ijamsville and the country beyond are lined with the First Brigade under Gen. Abercrombie. Towards the South, the road and roadsides swarm with supply trains and all the moving material, munitions, and men of a vast army; while the slopes of the Blue Ridge, on the West, glitter in the autumn sun with the emcamped host, composing the Third Brigade under General Williams. We seem to realize the fable of Cadmus, and a harvest of Dragon's teeth fills the fertile valley of the Monocacy with legions of armed men: the paraphernalia of grim-visaged war abound on every hand and its stern alarums resound on the palpating air. It is not a dream, but a palpable reality, whose fearful consequences are soon to fall with crushing force upon those authors of evil, who have so wantonly filled this Heaven-favored land with unnatural contention and the devastation of fire and sword. The Division of the Federal army, lately forming the "Muddy Branch camps" near Darnestown, have moved to this locality. The object of the movement hither is evidently to occupy a more eligible position for reserves, for a forward movement upon the rebels, or for Winter quarters as the case may be. In any event, they are welcome as the patriotic defenders of the Union and the Constitution, and if warm hearts and hospitable hands can give aid and comfort to the noble cause in which they have embarked, we bid them God Speed. The Major General, on whom devolves so much responsibility and in whose ability and resources such an abiding confidence is felt, is here too, to bear the Stars and stripes on to victory. His head quarters are at the house not long since occupied by one, now a traitor to his country, and more recently the lodging place of certain Tory members of the Legislature, who laboriously abused their trust, in the vain hope of convulsing Maryland and dragging her into the polluted slough of Secession. The various portions of the Major General's staff are quartered in other residences, and every vacant dwelling is now tenuated by martial inmates. The hotels and boarding houses are filled to repletion, and officers and their wives and children enlarge the domestic circle of may private families. Thanks to discipline, and the regard shown by those in authority for a loyal

community, good order prevails, no property is taken
without ample recompense; no rights are invaded; the
feeling of security is universal, and but for the martial
characteristics that dapple the scene, we could almost
persuade ourselves that the glad era of prosperity, which
preceded domestic treason, has been restored.

Another Frederick newspaper, the <u>Maryland Union</u>, printed this cryptic item on December 19, 1861.

LEFT FOR WILLIAMSPORT.- Capts. Cole and
Horner's Cavalry Companies left this city at 8 O'clock last
evening in haste for Williamsport. Something is out.

PART IV
THE PERSONALITIES

In researching the subject of this book, a number of the writers of the letters in the author's collection were found to be actual participants in the Potomac Home Brigade or in other units during the War. Some were prominent citizens in their respective communities.

Frederick W. Alexander of Baltimore became Captain of the Baltimore Battery of Light Artillery (Alexander's Battery) organized in the Summer of 1862.

Dr. Augustin A. Biggs of Sharpsburg was a practicing physician for 53 years. He was a well-known "strong Union Man," so much so that Confederate General Reynolds actually planned to capture Dr. Biggs, but failed. After the War, he was named Superintendent of the Antietam National Cemetery.

J. D. Bennett of Hagerstown was a prominent local member of the Union Party and a noted public speaker at Pro-Union rallies at which Francis Thomas and Lewis Fiery also spoke. The reader will note that in addition to the letter in the author's collection, two succeeding letters were discovered, and are quoted above.

Roger Ellsworth Cook, Captain of the Sharpsburg Rifles, entered the army on August 15, 1861, as Captain of Company A, First Regiment, Potomac Home Brigade. He was promoted to Major on February 6, 1863; Lieutenant

Colonel, November 23, 1863; Colonel, February 24, 1865. After the War, he settled in Hagerstown, Maryland.

William F. Craig enlisted on July 23, 1861 in the Second Maryland Regiment, Company E.

Lewis Dysche, Hancock, Maryland, was mustered in as Captain, Company F, Second Regiment, Potomac Home Brigade on August 26, 1861. He resigned on October 25, 1862.

James P. Lowell enlisted as a Private in the First Regiment, Company B, Potomac Home Brigade on September 6, 1861 and deserted on September 20, 1862.

Charles G. McClelland was enrolled as Captain, Company G, Second Regiment, Potomac Home Brigade on August 8, 1861. He resigned on March 31, 1862.

Jacob E. Myers served in Cole's Cavalry, Potomac Home Brigade for three years.

John H. Huntley, Frostburg, Maryland, was mustered in as Captain, Company C, Second Regiment, Potomac Home Brigade on July 20, 1861. He was promoted to Major on May 13, 1862 and mustered out , October 4, 1864.

Samuel G. Prather of Clearspring, Maryland, entered service on August 21, 1861 as Captain, Company F, First Regiment, Potomac Home Brigade. He died in Frederick on October 15, 1861. See the above obituary notice from the Frederick newspaper.

Horace Resley does not appear on any roster of the Potomac Home Brigade. However, four of the names listed in his letter of August 12, 1861, do appear. James C. Lynn, Levi Shaw, Samuel Shipley, and George Wigley are all listed as having served in the Second Regiment in various capacities.

James D. Roberts of Cumberland, Maryland, was enrolled as Captain, Company B, Second Regiment, Potomac Home Brigade on August 12, 1861. He left the army on December 3, 1862.

Alexander Shaw of Lonaconing, Maryland was enrolled on August 1, 1861, as Captain, Company A, Second Regiment, Potomac Home Brigade. He was promoted to Major, January 18, 1862, and resigned March 31, 1862.

Joseph M. Sudsburg, Baltimore, entered the service on September 18, 1861, as Captain, Company K, Second Maryland Regiment. In November, 1861, he was transferred to the Fourth Maryland Infantry (The German Rifles). He eventually rose to the rank of Colonel. In reading his letter one can very easily come to the conclusion that his name is "Tudsburg". After a discussion with a staff member at the Maryland Historical Society Library, who referred to him as Sudsburg, the Author was able to correct

176

his mistaken reading of the signature. See the Sudsburg letter.

George D. Summers enlisted on August 8, 1861, as a First Lieutenant, Company F, Second Regiment, Potomac Home Brigade. He replaced Lewis Dysche as Captain on December 9, 1862. Captain Summers was killed in action on October 7, 1863, at Summit Point, Virginia.

The following persons are prominently mentioned in this work and are worthy of note.

Francis (Frank) Thomas was one of the most colorful and eccentric individuals in Maryland history. Born on a farm named Montevue, in Frederick County near Petersville, on February 3, 1799, he received his education at St. Johns College in Annapolis. He studied law and was admitted to the Bar in 1820. His political career began with his election to the House of Delegates, the lower house in the Maryland legislature, in 1822, and in his rising to the position of Speaker in 1829. He served Western Maryland as a member of Congress from March 4, 1831, to March 4, 1841. On August 5, 1840, Thomas met in a duel, Mr. William Price, a member of the Washington County Bar, for a speech that Price delivered in Cumberland to which Mr. Thomas took offense. The duel took place across the Potomac on the road between Berkley Springs and Hancock, Maryland. At twelve paces, both men fired and missed. The friends of the combatants then intervened and effected an honorable end to the dispute. At the time this event occurred, Mr. Thomas was Chairman of the House Judiciary Committee. On June 8, 1841, at the age of 42, he married the 20 year old Sallie McDowell. The marriage seemed doomed from the start due to the age difference and what was described at the time as Thomas' "insane" jealousy. In November of 1841, Thomas was successful in his campaign for Governor. Shortly thereafter, severe difficulties arose between the Governor and Mrs. Thomas which escalated to the point when her Father, the Governor of Virginia, came to Thomas' home near Petersville and took his daughter home. Soon after this, Governor Thomas perpetrated an act, said at the time, as that of a "lunatic". Shortly before his term of office was to expire, he published a fifty page pamphlet in which he aired his version of his marital troubles and attacked the male members of his wife's family, especially her father and her uncle, Thomas Hart Benton, United States Senator from Missouri. As a result of this pamphlet being placed on the desk of each member of the House of Representatives and U. S. Senate, a libel suit was filed in the District of Columbia against Governor Thomas. In an attempt to avoid answering the suit, Thomas falsely accused the Honorable John Carroll Legrand of stealing property from his home and tried to institute impeachment proceedings against Legrand whom he had earlier appointed to the bench. The Governor hoped that he would be prevented from answering the summons in the law suit by the impeachment trial. In a speech before the legislature, the Governor almost incited violence on the part of Senator Benton, by expressing, in the strongest terms, his disdain for the male members of his wife's family. This was done in the presence of Mrs Thomas, her father, and Senator Benton, who were all seated in the chamber. The Senator rose from his seat and shouted that if the legislature would not protect him, " I will protect myself." The Speaker tried to call Governor Thomas to order, and the session broke up in chaos. These bizarre circumstances were said to have cost Francis Thomas the Presidency of the United States. The Democratic Candidate was virtually assured of election in the campaign of 1844. Thomas was considered a front runner for the nomination. The bitter dispute with his wife's family caused his father-in-law, Governor McDowell, a major power in the party, to induce the nominating committee not to put Thomas' name before the Democratic Convention in Baltimore. After a prolonged deadlock in which there were numerous ballots, the first surprise, or "Dark Horse," candidate was finally nominated. That person was James K. Polk of Tennessee who defeated Henry Clay, the Whig Candidate. In 1846 the Maryland legislature passed a bill granting a divorce to Governor Thomas. Attempting a comeback, Thomas ran as an independent candidate for Congress against the Democratic Nominee but was narrowly defeated. Thereafter, he retired to his law practice in Frederick. In 1860 he spoke at a number of Union rallies and was elected to Congress in a special election in 1861. He directed the recruiting of 3,000 volunteers for the Potomac Home Brigade. His second stint in Congress expired in 1869 at the age of 70. As a delegate to the Maryland Constitutional Convention of 1864, Mr. Thomas was the author of the provision which abolished slavery in the state. In recognition of past service, President Grant appointed Governor Thomas to the post of Collector of the Internal Revenue for Maryland. In 1872 the President named him Minster to Peru where he served until 1875. Francis Thomas retired to a cabin in Garrett County, Maryland. On January 22, 1876, while walking on the B. & O. Railroad tracks nearby, he was run over by a locomotive and killed instantly. He was buried in the cemetery of St. Marks Church near Petersville. The epitaph on his tombstone was self-composed.

"Ex-Gov. Francis Thomas, born February 3, 1799, died January, 1876, son of Col. John Thomas and his wife, Eleanor McGill. The author of the measure which gave to Maryland the Constitution of 1864 and thereby gave freedom to 90,000 human beings."

Major Richard Somers Smith of the Regular U. S. Army was a native of Pennsylvania and entered the United States Military Academy July 1, 1829. He was commissioned a brevet second lieutenant in the Second Infantry on July 1, 1834. On October 19, 1836, Smith resigned. He re-entered the Army on December 31, 1840, as a Second Lieutenant assigned to the Seventh Infantry and was promoted to First Lieutenant on April 19, 1846. He was transferred to the Fourth Artillery August 31, 1848, and again resigned January 13, 1856. On May 14, 1861, Smith was commissioned Major in the Twelfth Infantry, and on July 25, 1861, he was detached as Mustering Officer for the Potomac Home Brigade in Frederick, Maryland. He was serving in this capacity, as we know from letters and newspaper articles cited above, during the period of time encompassed by this book. Major Smith served until May 30, 1863, the date of his third and final resignation. He died on January 23, 1877.

Colonel William P. Maulsby, Commander of the First Regiment, was founder and owner of the <u>Democratic Union</u>, a newspaper published in Frederick in 1853. He later sold the paper and the new owner renamed it the <u>Maryland Union</u>. Maulsby was a practicing attorney in Frederick during the 1850's until enlisting in the service. He served for three years, leading his troops in the battles of Charlestown, Harper's Ferry, Martinsburg, Gettysburg, and Monocacy. At Harper's Ferry, he had the dubious honor of surrendering his entire Regiment to Stonewall Jackson during the campaign leading to the Battle of Antietam. At Gettysburg, his troops participated in the fight at Culp's Hill where he was slightly wounded and afterward was cited for his leadership. After the War, the Colonel resumed his law practice in Frederick taking his son William, Jr. into the firm. William, Jr. served with his father in the First Regiment, enlisting in August, 1861, as a private in Company G, and later rose to First Lieutenant and Adjutant in Regimental Headquarters. Colonel Maulsby was appointed Chief Judge of the Sixth Circuit by Governor Bowie and also served as a member of the Maryland Court of Appeals.

Colonel Thomas Johns, a subject of two of the letters in the author's collection, was born March 5, 1812, in

Georgetown, D.C. He graduated as Cadet Captain from the U. S. Military Academy at West Point on July 1, 1833. Due to ill health, he resigned from the army on August 31, 1841, and found employment as a clerk for the Maryland Mining Company in Cumberland, Maryland. In 1855 Johns, established a hardware store in Cumberland which he continued to own until his retirement in 1872. He was commissioned Colonel of the Second Regiment, Potomac Home Brigade on October 11, 1861. Again, his health forced him to resign from service on January 1, 1862, when he was succeeded by Robert Bruce. Colonel Johns died June 17, 1882.

Robert Bruce, of Cumberland, Maryland and mentioned in the letter from George A. Pierce, was a senior accountant in the Bank of Allegany for a number of years. Elected in 1836, he served as a member of the Maryland House of Delegates. Mr. Bruce was highly active in recruiting the Second Regiment of the Potomac Home Brigade, of which he eventually became Colonel, and actively served as such to the end of the War. Following the War, he was elected Judge of the Orphan's Court in 1874. He served in this capacity sixteen years until his death in 1890. His ancestry is reputed to be traceable to Robert The Bruce, King of Scotland.

General Edward Otho Cresap Ord is the subject of the letter of Francis Thomas quoted above. He was a direct descendant of Colonel Daniel Delaney Cresap of the Continental Army in the Revolutionary War. He was born near Cumberland, Maryland on October 18, 1818. After attending West Point and graduating in 1839, Ord was assigned to the Third U. S. Artillery. He served in the Seminole War, the Mexican War under General Taylor, and later in wars with the Indians in California. In 1861 he was given command of all volunteer units serving along the Potomac River, of which the Potomac Home Brigade was one. Promoted to Major General in 1862, he was ordered to Mississippi. He commanded the Thirteenth Army Corps which participated in the Capture of Corinth and Vicksburg and in the campaign against Richmond, he was in command of the Eighteenth Corps and all of the Department of Virginia at the evacuation of the city in 1865. Following the assassination of President Lincoln, he refused to follow an order of Secretary of War Stanton to arrest every Confederate officer in Richmond. Ord wired the Secretary that none of the officers was violating his parole; therefore, he would not arrest them. Upon hearing this, General Grant telegraphed Stanton that he fully supported General Ord in his stand. General Ord, second in command under Grant, was the commander of the troops directly in front of General Robert E. Lee's army at Appomattox and was the officer to whom Lee sent the white flag of surrender. After retiring from active service, General Ord died on July 22, 1883, in Havana, Cuba.

Daniel Blocher, a prominent citizen of Cumberland, was born in that city in 1809. In 1832, he became proprietor and editor of the *Maryland Advocate*, a Democratic newspaper, until 1838 when he sold the organ. While running the paper, he studied law and was admitted to the bar. In the legislative terms of 1837 and 1838, Mr. Blocher was a member of the General Assembly of Maryland. In 1841, he was appointed Register of Wills in Allegany County and served until 1846. He then resigned and was elected State Senator. Mr. Blocher was appointed inspector of the cattle scales in Baltimore in 1854. In 1861 he was made Baltimore recruiting officer for the First Regiment, Potomac Home Brigade. Shortly thereafter, he became Quartermaster of the First Regiment and served for three years. After the War, he moved back to Cumberland and was appointed Justice of the Peace for Allegany County. He served in this office until his death in 1882.

George R. Dennis was a prominent farmer and business man in Frederick County having settled there in 1853. He was born in Somerset County on March 15, 1831, and was educated at Dickinson College. A staunch Union supporter, he entered the service as Lieutenant-Colonel of the First Regiment, November 28, 1861. He resigned from the army on September 11, 1862. In 1863 he was appointed to the Board of Directors of the Baltimore and Ohio Railroad. In addition, Mr. Dennis held the position of President of the Central National Bank of Frederick, member of the Board of Visitors of the Maryland School for the Deaf in Frederick, and member of the Board of Managers of the Frederick County Agricultural Society. He was owner and manager of several large farms in Frederick County. Twice married, he fathered eleven children. His first wife was Alice McPherson, daughter of Colonel John McPherson and great-granddaughter of Thomas Johnson. Following her death, Mr. Dennis married her sister, Fanny. Colonel Dennis died at his farm, Hampton, near Urbana on August 23, 1902.

Secretary of War Simon Cameron

Massachusetts Commandery Military Order of the Loyal Legion

and the U. S. Military History Institute

186

Major General Nathaniel Banks

Massachusetts Commandery Military Order of the loyal legion

and the U. S. Military history Institute

General E. O. C. Ord

Massachusetts Commandery Military Order of the Loyal Legion

and the U. S. Militaary History Institute

General Bradley T. Johnson, C.S. A.

Massachusetts Commandery Military Order of the Loyal Legion

and the U. S. Military History Institute

Saint Marks Church Petersville, Maryland site of Francis Thomas' grave

Photo by Keith O. Gary

Front of Francis Thomas' gravestone.

Photo by Keith O. Gary

The author of the measure
which gave to Maryland the
Constitution of 1864, and
therby gave freedom to ninety
thousand human beings.

Rear of Francis Thomas' gravestone.

Photo by Keith O. Gary

Inventory of the effects of Private William T. Slack deceased. Late of Company C. 1st Maryland Regiment of the Potomac Home Brigade Volunteers. who enlisted at Baltimore City, Maryland, on the second day of September 1861. and who died at Camp Worman Frederick County Maryland. on the twenty fifth day of December 1861. Cause Congestion of the Brain and Lungs.

Quantity	Articles	Location	Comdg Officers Remarks.
1	Pair of Blankets.	Camp	The within named Private
1	Over Coat.	Worman	William T. Slack. was buried in his
1	Pair of Woolen Hose.	Frederick.	uniform, suit of Clothes and the rem-
1	Pair of Cotton Hose.	County.	-ainder of his effects passed in to the
1	Cap.	Maryland	possession of the Regt. Q. Mr. subject to
2	Set under Shirts.		the order of his Father William S.
2	Pair of White Muslin Drawers.		Slack. who lives in Baltimore City
2	Shirt Collars		Md. who by the Laws of Md. is entitled
			to all the personal estate of Deceased.

I certify that the above Inventory is correct.

William T. ____ Captain of
Company C. 1st Maryland Regiment of the
Potomac Home Brigade, Volunteers.

Inventory of the Effects of Private William T. Slack

The Gary Collection

193

Final Statement of account of William T. Slack, deceased, late of Company C. 1st Maryland Regiment of the Potomac Home Brigade Volunteers, of Pay and Clothing received and indebtedness to the United States, from the second day of September 1861. the day of his enlistment to the twenty fifth day of December 1861. the date of his Death,

Statement of accounts
With the United States

	Dr.	Cr.
To 1 Pair of Blankets	3.50	
" 1 Over Coat.	7.50	
" 1 Sack coat and Pantloons.	7.50	
" 2 Pair of Drawers a 75¢	1.50	
" 2 Under Shirts @ 75¢	1.50	
" 2 Pair of Stockings (a 31¢	62	
" 1 Cap	1.25	
" 1 Pair of Shoes	2.00	25.37
To Pay from the second day of September 1861. the date of his enlistment to the thirty first day of October 1861. the date when last Paid.		25.56
To Pay from the second day of September 1861. the date of his enlistment to the twenty fifth day of December 1861. the date of his death at $ 13. per month.		47.77
To Clothing allowance @ $3.50 per Month of Said dates		13.72
		62.50
To Ballance due William T. Slack.		1.60 38
	$50.93	$50.93

I certify that the above Statement of accounts is correct.

William T. Faithful Captain of
Company C. 1st Maryland Regiment of the
Potomac Home Brigade.
Volunteers.

Final Statement of Account of Private William T. Slack

The Gary Collection

Inventory of the effects of Private Joseph Tobin deceased. late of Company C 1st Maryland Regiment of the Potomac Home Brigade. Volunteers. who enlisted at Baltimore City Maryland, on the Second day of September 1861. and who died at Regimental Hospital, Camp Worman, Frederick County Maryland the Twenty fifth day of January 1863. Cause Abscess on the Spine—

No.	Articles.		Commanding Officers Remarks
1	Pair of Blankets.	Joseph	The within named Private
1	Over Coat.	Worman	Joseph Tobin was buried in his
1	Razor and Razor Strop.	Frederick	Uniform suit of Clothes. and the re-
1	Tin Cup.	County	mainder of his effects passed into
1	Cap.	Maryland	the possession of the Regimental
1	Pair of Woollen Hose		Quarter Master subject to the
1	Towel.		order of his wife who lives in
2	Blue Check Shirts.		Baltimore City Maryland. who
2	Pair of Knit Drawers.		by the laws of Maryland, is
1	Knit Shirt.		entitled to all the personal
1	Pair of Shoes.		estate of deceased.
1	Pair of Citizens Pantaloons.		
1	Needle wallet.		

I certify that the above Inventory is correct.

William T. Fairthorne Captain of
Company C 1st Maryland Regt.
of the Potomac Home Brigade.
Volunteers.

Inventory of the Effects of Private Joseph Tobin

The Gary Collection

195

Final Statement of account of Private Joseph Tobin deceased. late of Company C 1st Maryland Regiment of the Potomac Home Brigade Volunteers of Pay and Clothing received from and indebtedness to the United States from the second day of September 1861 the day of his enlistment to the twenty fifth day of January 1862 the date of his death.   Statement of Accounts
              With the United States.

		Drs	Crs
To 1 Pair of Blankets	3.50		
" 1 Over Coat	7.50		
" 1 Jacket coat and Pantloons	7.50		
" 2 Pair of Drawers @ 75¢	1.50		
" 2 Under Shirts @ 75¢	1.50		
" 2 Pair of Stockings @ 31½	.63		
" 1 Cap	1.25		
" 2 Pair of Shoes @ $2	4.00	35.38	
To Pay from the second day of September 1861 the day of his enlistment to the thirty first of October 1861 the date when last paid		25.56	
To Pay from the second day of September 1861 the day of his enlistment to the twenty fifth day of January 1862 the date of his death @ $13 per Month			62.82
To Clothing allowance @ $3.50 per Month of said dates			16.57½
			$79.49½
To Balance due Joseph Tobin			28.55½
		$50.9¼	$50.94

I certify that the above Statement of Account is Correct.

                    William T. Carter Captain of
                        Company C 1st Maryland Regiment
                        of the Potomac Home Brigade.
                                            Volunteers.

Final Statement of Account of Private Joseph Tobin

The Gary Collection

196

Final Statement of account of the late John M. Davis a Private of Company E 1st Maryland Regt Potomac Home Brigade Volunteers of Pay and Clothing received from and indebtedness to the United States since the 6th day of September 1861 the day of his enlistment to the 30th day of December 1861 the day of his death

Statement of account

With the United States   Dr   Cr

To 1 pr Blankets		$3.50
" 1 Sack Coat and Pants		7.50
" 1 Over Coat		7.50
" 2 Shirts	1.06½	2.13
" 2 Prs Drawers	75	1.50
" 2 Pas ½ Hose	31	.62
" 1 Cap		1.25
" 1 Pr Shoes		2.00
" 1 " do		1.94
" 1 " do		2.00
" 1 " ½ Hose		.31

Total amount of Clothing drawn and value $30.25

To Pay from 6th day of September 1861 the date of his enlistment to the 30th day of December 1861 the day of his death @ $13. or pr Month $49.84

of said date to Clothing allowance @ $3.50 pr Month of said date $13.43

$63.27

$ 30.25   30.25

To Balance due John M. Davis   33.02

I Certify that the above Statement and account is Correct and just William H. H. Seal Capt E Company E 1st Maryland Regt Potomac Home Brigade of Volunteers

Final Statement of Account of Private John M. Davis

The Gary Collection

Inventory of the effects of Private James H. Clark, deceased, late of Co-
-mpany C, 1st Maryland Regiment of the Potomac Home Brigade Voluntiers,
who entisted at Baltimore City Maryland, on the second day of Sept-
-ember 1861, and who died at Camp Thomas Frederick City Maryland, on
the twenty second day of November 1861 Cause Inflamation of the Bowels.

Quantity.	Articles.	Location.	Cond'g Officers. Remarkes.
1	Pair of Blankets	Camp	The within named Private
1	Over Coat.	Thomas	James H. Clark, was buried in his
1	Pair of Drawers.	Frederick	Uniform and the remainder of his
1	Pair of Hose	City	effects passed into the posession of the
1	Cotton under Shirt.	Maryland	Reg'l. Q.M. subject to the order of
2	White Dress Shirts.		his wife Elizabeth Pauline
1	Cap.		Clark, who lives in Baltimore City
			Md. who by the Laws of Maryland
			is entitled to all the Personal es-
			-tate of Deceased.

I certify that the above Inventory is correct.

William ——— Captain of.
Company C. 1st Maryland Regiment of the
Potomac Home Brigade. Voluntiers,

Inventory of the Effects of Private James H. Clark

The Gary Collection

198

Inventory of the effects of Private George W. Misner deceased, late of Company I, 1st Maryland Regiment of the Potomac Home Brigade Volunteers, who enlisted at Frederick City, Md., on the seventeenth day of December 1861; and who died at his residence near Liberty, Frederick County, Md., the twentieth day of January 1862. Cause — Measles.

number or quantity	Articles.	Location.	Commanding Officers Remarks.
1	Cap	Camp Worman Frederick County. Maryland	The within named Private George W. Misner was buried in his Uniform and the remainder of his effects passed into the possession of his wife who lives near Liberty, Frederick County, Md, who by the laws of Maryland is entitled to all the personal estate of deceased
1	Pair of Shoes		

I certify that the above Inventory is correct,

Walter Saunders Captain of Company I, 1st Maryland Regiment of the Potomac Home Brigade Volunteers.

Inventory of the Effects of Private George W. Misner

The Gary Collection

Final Statement of account of Private George W. Misner deceased, late of Company J, 1st Maryland Regiment of the Potomac Home Brigade Volunteers, of pay and clothing received from and indebtedness to the United States, from the seventeenth day of December, 1861. the day of his enlistment to the twentieth day of January. 1862. the date of his Death.

Statement of Accounts
With the United States.

		Dr.	Cr.
To 1 Pair of Blankets.	$3.50		
1 Over Coat.	7.75		
1 Sack-coat and Pantaloons.	8.00		
2 Pairs of Drawers @ 75c.	1.50		
2 Under Shirts @ 75c.	1.50		
2 Pairs of Stockings @ 30c.	60		
1 Cap.	1.25		
1 Pair of Shoes.	1.75	$26.85.	
To Pay from the Seventeenth day of December 1861. the date of his enlistment to the twentieth of January, 1862 the date of his Death. @ $13. per month.			$14.30
To Clothing allowance at $3.50 per month, of said dates.			3.85
			$18.15
Total due the United States.			8.70
		$26.85.	$26.85

I certify that the above Statement of accounts is Correct.

Walter Saunders Captain of
Company J, 1st Maryland Regiment
of the Potomac Home Brigade.
Volunteers.

Final Statement of Account of Private George W. Misner

The Gary Collection

200

Lovers Rock Cemetery as viewed facing west with the rock on the upper left.

Photo by Keith O. Gary

Lovers Rock Cemetery as viewed from the rock facing east.

Photo by Keith O. Gary

Head Quarters, Genl Banks Division
Frederick City, Md. Jan 3rd 1862

General Order
No. 19

On and after this date, all mounted messengers found riding their horses faster than the exigency of the Order demands, shall be punished for violating "General Orders," relating thereto. Henceforth, all Orders and Despatches, will be marked on the wrapper the pace at which they are to be carried; and any deviation from the Order will be severely punished.

By Command of
Major General Banks
R. Morris Copeland
Asst. Adjt. General

Col. W.P. Maulsby
1st Maryland "Home Brigade"

General Order Number 19 regulating the speed of mounted messengers

The Gary Collection

PART V
THE VOLUNTEERS

The list of names which follows is a compilation of the men who first answered the call. Those who enlisted after December, 1861, have been omitted. A complete but somewhat inaccurate list can be found in The History and Roster of Maryland Volunteers. The volunteers are listed by name, rank, and date of enlistment.

FIRST REGIMENT
POTOMAC HOME BRIGADE
COMPANY A

Bamford, Henry A., Private, August 15, 1861.

Bell, Jacob, Private, August 15, 1861.

Bender, Augustus, Private, September 19, 1861.

Bender, John, Private, August 15, 1861.

Benner, Daniel, Private, August 15, 1861.

Benner, Joseph, Private, August 15, 1861.

Bond, George W., Private, August 15, 1861.

Bowers, Daniel, Private, August 15, 1861.

Brown, Josephus, Private, August 15, 1861.

Caldwell, William, Private, August 15, 1861.

Carr, Samuel M., Private, August 15, 1861

Cook, Alexander H., Private, August 15,1861.

Dailey, William, Private, August 15, 1861.

Delaney, James T., Private, August 15, 1861.

Delaney, John F., Private, August 15, 1861.

Dreuner, David F., Private, August 15, 1861.

Farling, Jonathan J., Private, August 15, 1861.

Fisher, John W., Private, August 15, 1861.

Fiser, Elias L., Private, August 15, 1861.

Gift, Augustus, Private, August 15, 1861.

Gift, John, Private, August 15, 1861.

Gift, Martin, August 15, 1861.

Glass, Peter, Private, August 15, 1861.

Glass, William, Private, August 15, 1861.

Gray, John, Private, August 15, 1861.

Gray, John W., Private, August 15, 1861.

Greenwalt, Joseph, Private, August 15, 1861.

Grimm, Jacob M. L., Private, August 15, 1861.

Grooms, James, Private, August 15, 1861.

Hebb, Richard H., Private, August 15, 1861.

Hemphill, Henry, Private, August 15, 1861.

Hemphill, William, Private, August 15, 1861.

Hewett, Abraham, Private, August 15, 1861.

Hewett, Daniel, Private, August 15, 1861.

Highbarger, Alfred, Private, August 15, 1861.

Houser, Barney, Private, August 15, 1861.

Jackson, Jonathan W., Private, August 15, 1861.

Jackson, Joseph A., Private, August 15, 1861.

Johnson, Jonathan P., Private, August 15, 1861.

Knot, Franklin, Private, August 15, 1861.

Kuhn, John, Private, August 15, 1861.

Keedy, Thomas J., Private, August 15, 1861.

Marrow, Thomas J., Private, August 15, 1861.

Miller, Samuel, Private, August 15, 1861.

Moore, James, Private, August 15, 1861.

Moore, John, Private, August 15, 1861.

Moore, John F., Private, August 15, 1861.

Moore, Ridgley, Private, August 15, 1861.

Mose, Alfred, Private, August 15, 1861.

Mose, Daniel, Private, August 15, 1861.

Mose, Jacob, Private August 15, 1861.

Murray, Charles T., Private, August 15, 1861.

Noland, Michael, Private, August 15, 1861.

Nuse, John, Private, August 15, 1861.

Nuse, Joseph W., Private, August 15, 1861.

Nuse, William, Private, August 15, 1861.

O'Brien, Dennis, Private, August 15, 1861.

Peacher, Oliver, Private, August 15, 1861.

Pennell, Hezekiah C., Private, August 15, 1861.

Porter, Charles W., Private, August 15, 1861.

Price, Benjamin F., Private, August 15, 1861.

Reynolds, George H., Private, August 15, 1861.

Rohrer, Henry C., Private, August 15, 1861.

Roullett, Jonathan W., Private, August 15, 1861.

Sandman, Benjamin F., Private, August 15, 1861.

Saylor, Edward E., Private, August 15, 1861.

Saylor, Henry, Private, August 15, 1861.

Seaman, James, Private, August 15, 1861.

Shaw, Charles R., Private, August 15, 1861.

Spong, Elias, Private, August 15, 1861.

Spong, John L., Private, August 15, 1861.

Spong, Mathias, Private, August 15, 1861.

Stippy, Simon, Private, August 15, 1861.

Stride, Rufus, Private, August 15, 1861.

Thomas, Jasper N., Private, August 15, 1861.

Wilson, Thomas L., Private, August 15, 1861.

Winks, Thomas, Private, August 15, 1861.

Wood, Robert, Private, August 15, 1861.

COMPANY B

Anthony, Michael A., Private, September 6, 1861.

Albert, Nathan O., Private, November 12, 1861.

Aldridge, William A., Private, September 6, 1861.

Baker, Augustus, Private, September 6, 1861.

Baltzel, Robert C., Private, November 13, 1861.

Bankard, Jonathan E., Private, September 6, 1861.

Bell, Alfred R., Private, September 6, 1861.

Best, Adam, Private, September 6, 1861.

Bowser, Levi, Private, September 6, 1861.

Brightwell, Alonzo, Private, September 6, 1861.

Cahill, Edward, Private, September 6, 1861.

Chappell, William H., Private, September 6, 1861.

Chilcote, George P., Private, September 6, 1861.

Creamer, George W., Private, September 6, 1861.

Crum, Jonathan W., Jr., Private, September 6, 1861.

Dayhoff, Peter, Private, September 6, 1861.

Degrange, Henry C., Private, September 6, 1861.

Edwards, Henry C., Private, September 6, 1861.

Fisher, George W., Private, September 6, 1861.

Fletcher, William L., Private, September 6, 1861.

Gray, Peter H., Private, September 6, 1861.

Green, John W., Private, September 6, 1861.

Groff, William S., Private, September 6, 1861.

Hargate, Charles E., Private, September 6, 1861.

Harn, Jesse, Private, September 6, 1861.

Hartman, Christian, Private, September 6, 1861.

Hays, William F., Private, September 6, 1861.

Heffner, James E., Private, September 6, 1861.

Heim, William H., Private, September 6, 1861.

Hesson, Alpheus, Private, September 6, 1861.

Hoffman, James A., Private, September 6, 1861.

Houck, Lewis H., Private, September 6, 1861.

Hudson, James B., Private, September 6, 1861.

Hunt, Henry, Private, September 6, 1861.

Kauffman, Henry, Private, September 6, 1861.

Keller, James D., Private, September 6, 1861.

Keller, Robert F., Private, September 6, 1861.

Kemper, Henry, Private, September 6, 1861.

Kelley, John, Private, September 6, 1861.

Lappan, Wellerton, Private, September 6, 1861.

Lowell, James P., Private, September 6, 1861.

Lugenbill, Jacob A., Private, September 6, 1861.

Luttman, George W., Private, September 23, 1861.

Lynch, James, Private, September 6, 1861.

Mackey, Horrace H., Private, September 6, 1861.

Manning, Lewis P., Private, September 17, 1861.

McBride, Dennis, Private, September 6, 1861.

Miller, George F., Private, September 6, 1861.

Mills, Andrew, Private, September 6, 1861.

Mitchell, Robert W., Private, September 6, 1861.

Moffett, William P., Private, September 6, 1861.

Neal, John F., Private, September 6, 1861.

Oursler, Charles W., Private, September 6, 1861.

Pilcher, Charles R., Private, September 6, 1861.

Pool, George W., Private, September 6, 1861.

Reisinger, Charles, Private, September 6, 1861.

Rice, Amos, Private, September 6, 1861.

Rickett, Andrew, Private, September 6, 1861.

Rinehart, Charles E., Private, September 6, 1861.

Shade, Henry, Private, September 6, 1861.

Smith, Thomas, Private, September 6, 1861.

Sparrow, Thomas, Private, September 6, 1861.

Stockman, David L., Private, September 6, 1861.

Stockman, Joseph G., Private, September 6, 1861.

Stouffer, Peter, Private, September 6, 1861.

Stride, George W., Private, September 6, 1861.

Tharp, William, Private, September 6, 1861.

Thomas, John P. G., Private, September 6, 1861.

Thomas, Wilber F., Private, September 6, 1861.

Trayer, David, Private, September 6, 1861.

Troxell, Zephaniah L., Private, November 20, 1861.

Wagner, Daniel A., Private, September 6, 1861.

Wagner, George D., Private, September 6, 1861.

Wagner, John A., Private, September 6, 1861.

Wagner, Joseph E., Private, September 6, 1861.

Warner, Charles A., Private, September 6, 1861.

Wheeler, Joseph A., Private, September 6, 1861.

Willcomb, Jerome, Private, September 6, 1861.

Yeakle, Andrew, Private, September 6, 1861.

Yingling, William H., Private, September 6, 1861.

Zahn, George A., Private, November 19, 1861.

COMPANY C

Barnes, Robert C., Jr., Corporal, August 29, 1861.

Battee, Samuel, Sergeant, August 29, 1861.

Baughman, Samuel W., Private, September 6, 1861.

Bell, John W., Private, August 29, 1861.

Bek, John, Private, August 29, 1861.

Birkbeck, Alexander H., Private, September 2, 1861.

Bowers, Jonathan Lee, Corporal, September 2, 1861.

Boyd, Benjamin F., Private, August 29, 1861.

Brown, Cornelius, Jr., Sergeant, August 29, 1861.

Brown, Samuel T., Private, September 6, 1861.

Brown, William G., Private, August 29, 1861.

Brown, William H., Corporal, August 29, 1861.

Burris, Edward, Private, August 29, 1861.

Clark, James H., Private, September 2, 1861.

Connor, Richard J. K., Private, September 2, 1861.

Cook, Thomas, Sergeant, August 29, 1861.

Coster, Joseph, Private, August 29, 1861.

Dulaney, Joseph F., Private, September 3, 1861.

Dutrow, William E., Private, September 4, 1861.

Fuller, George W., Private, September 12, 1861.

Gibson, John W., Private, August 29, 1861.

Gill, Joseph C., Private, August 29, 1861.

Gourley, George, Private, October 24, 1861.

Gosnell, Moses, Private, September 3, 1861.

Haigis, John, Corporal, September 4, 1861.

Hainrich, Albert, Private, September 16, 1861.

Hainrich, Constant, Private, September 16, 1861.

Hall, Francis A., Private, September 12, 1861.

Harris, George M., Private, September 12, 1861.

High, George W., Private, September 12, 1861.

Holtz, George G., Corporal, August 29, 1861.

Jamison, Robert, Private, August 29, 1861.

Keith, James, Private, August 29, 1861.

Keough, Henry M., Private, August 29, 1861.

Kinnersley, William T., Private, September 4, 1861.

Latta, Joshua W., Private, August 29, 1861.

Lindenthal, John, Private, September 13, 1861.

Lisle, John D., Private, September 2, 1861.

Lowdenslager, John w., Private, August 29, 1861.

Lucas, Valentine, Private, September 12, 1861.

Lutz, John G., Private, September 16, 1861.

McCauley, Daniel H., Private, August 29, 1861.

McDonald, Jonathan A., Private, September 2, 1861.

Miller, Henry, Private, September 12, 1861.

Mills, William, Jr., Private, August 29, 1861.

Moffett, John N., Private, August 29, 1861.

Morrison, Charles H. S., Corporal, August 29, 1861.

Myers, Anthony, Private, August 29, 1861.

Newton, Isaac H., Private, August 29, 1861.

Norris, John, Private, September 3, 1861.

Patterson, Samuel W., Teamster, August 29, 1861.

Penniman, Horace, Private, August 29, 1861.

Poston, Jonathan H., Private, September 4, 1861.

Read, Joseph E., Private, September 3, 1861.

Renoff, George W., Private, August 29, 1861.

Roberts, Charles H., Private, August 29, 1861.

Saunders, William W., Private, November 11, 1861.

Schafer, Jonathan A., Private, September 12, 1861.

Schafer, Robert, Musician, August 29, 1861.

Sherwood, William J., Private, August 29, 1861.

Shields, George W., Private, September 5, 1861.

Shipley, George W., Private, August 29, 1861.

Shriver, Daniel C., Private, August 29, 1861.

Slack, William T., Private, September 2, 1861.

Smith, Charles E., Corporal, August 29, 1861.

Stall, John, Private, September 16, 1861.

Stoll, Leopold, Sergeant, August 29, 1861.

Strong, George W., Private, August 29, 1861.

Strong, William, Private, August 29, 1861.

Tobin, Joseph, Private, September 2, 1861.*

Turner, Edwin F., Private, September 3, 1861.

Wain, William L., Private, August 29, 1861.

Whorton, George D., Private, August 29, 1861.

Wild, Henry C., Private, September 13, 1861.

Willmer, Gideon L., Private, August 29, 1861.

Willmer, William B., Private, August 29, 1861.

Woodward, Francis D., Private, August 29, 1861.

Wren, Thomas, Private, September 12, 1861.

*Wilmer and Jarrett list this name as Tobias. However, the reader can judge for himself by closely examining the two documents which are presented in facsimile above. The enlistment date and the date of death exactly coincide, and I believe the name is clearly spelled Tobin in these two documents.

COMPANY D

Andrews, Samuel S., Private, September 18, 1861.

Barthalow, Prestley, Private, September 18, 1861.

Barger, Columbus, Private, October 1, 1861.

Baxter, Francis, Private, October 1, 1861.

Bellis, Roger, Sergeant, October 1, 1861.

Bellison, Milton L., Private, December 13, 1861.

Bender, Jacob, Private, August 16, 1861.

Booth, William H., Private, October 1, 1861.

Brill, George, Private, September 4, 1861.

Butler, James, Private, October 25, 1861.

Boyd, Charles H., Private, September 18, 1861.

Carnes, William, Private, September 18, 1861.

Chambers, Michael, Private, September 18, 1861.

Church, William H., Private, September 18, 1861.

Cleggett, Jonathan T., Private, October 25, 1861.

Colbert, Samuel, Private, December 13, 1861.

Cosgrove, Jesse D., Private, October 1, 1861.

Crabb, Jeremiah, Private, December 13, 1861.

Crum, Isaac L., Corporal, September 18, 1861.

Donaldson, Donald, Private, October 25, 1861.

Earp, Wilson L., Private, September 18, 1861.

Edmonds, Thomas, Private, September 18, 1861.

Engle, George, Private, September 18, 1861.

Fante, George C., Private, September 18, 1861.

Fisher, Joseph W., Private, September 18, 1861.

Ford, John J., Private, September 18, 1861.

Ford Stephen, Private, October 1, 1861.

Frey, John M., Private, September 18, 1861.

Fry, Daniel, Private, August 15, 1861.

Gaswell, Moses, Private, September 13, 1861.

Giles, Edward, Private, September 18, 1861.

Gourley, George, Private, October 24, 1861.

Hahn, Abrom J., Private, September 18, 1861.

Hahn, Michael J., Private, September 18, 1861.

Harris, George H., Private, September 13, 1861.

Harrison, Andrew A., Private, September 18, 1861.

Harper, Lloyd M., Corporal, October 1, 1861.

Hemphile, Alexander, Private, October 1, 1861.

Hemphill, Henry, Private, August 15, 1861.

Hissong, Samuel H., Private, October 1, 1861.

Holbrooks, William H., Private, October 15, 1861.

Ingram, Jonathan W., Private, August 15, 1861.

James, John, Private, August 15, 1861.

Johnson, Jonathan H., Private, August 15, 1861.

Kuhn, Leander H., Corporal, September 18, 1861.

Labadie, Joseph E., Private, September 14, 1861.

Lambaugh, Charles A., Private, September 18, 1861.

Lewis, Charles A., Private, September 18, 1861.

Lorentz, Lloyd M., Private, October 1, 1861.

Lowrey, Matthew J., Private, October 15, 1861.

McDaniel, George, Private, September 18, 1861.

Martin, James, Private, October 1, 1861.

Martin, Warren T., Sergeant, October 15, 1861.

Mitchell, Henry T., Private, October 15, 1861.

Misner, William H., Private, September 18, 1861.

Morgan, Lawson, Private, August 15, 1861.

Noggle, Samuel, Private, August 15, 1861.

Nuse, Daniel, Private, August 15, 1861.

Nuse, Hezekiah, Private, August 15, 1861.

Parrish, Henry M., Private, September 18, 1861.

Pennel, George M., Private, August 15, 1861.

Pennel, Isaac, Private, September 18, 1861.

Poole, William H., Private, December 13, 1861.

Porter, Levi, Private, August 15, 1861.

Price, Thomas, Private, August 15, 1861.

Richards, John, Private, September 18, 1861.

Rippen, John F., Private, September 18, 1861.

Seidel, Gottlieb, Private, December 13, 1861.

Schultz, William H., Private, October 10, 1861.

Shriner, Lewis E., Sergeant, October 1, 1861.

Smyser, William H., Private, October 10, 1861.

Stickells, John, Private, September 6, 1861.

Tabler, Franklin C., Corporal, September 18, 1861.

Walker, John T., Private, September 18, 1861.

Wellen, Ambrose, Private, September 18, 1861.

Webster, Daniel F., Private, December 23, 1861.

Wellen, Amos F., Corporal, September 18, 1861.

Wigley, William A., Corporal, September 18, 1861.

Wilhelm, Reason J., Private, August 15, 1861.

Wilhide, Daniel, Private, October 1, 1861.

Wilhide, Martin H., Private, September 18, 1861.

COMPANY E

Alsoup, Jonathan H., Private, December 15, 1861.

Andrew, Jeremiah, Private, September 14, 1861.

Andrew, William, Private, September 14, 1861.

Beard, John, Private, October 1, 1861.

Bennix, William C., Private, October 1, 1861.

Besore, Oscar, Private, December 13, 1861.

Bickley, Christian F., Private, October 1, 1861.

Biershing, Jonathan H., Private, September 14, 1861.

Bohn, Henry C., Private, September 14, 1861.

Bowers, Daniel R., Private, October 1, 1861.

Boyer, John, Private, December 13, 1861.

Boyer, Peter, Private, October 1, 1861.

Bragonier, David F., Private, August 10, 1861.

Bridges, Clarence W., Private, November 30, 1861.

Buckey, David D., Private, September 6, 1861.

Carn, Thomas E., Private, September 14, 1861.

Cline, John, Private, October 25, 1861.

Cline, Levi, Private, October 25, 1861.

Coffman, James H., Private, September 14, 1861.

Cosgrove, Jesse D., Private, September 14, 1861.

Cramer, Jonathan H., Private, September 14, 1861.

Crumbaugh, William C., Private, September 14, 1861.

Davis, John M., Private, September 14, 1861.

Dell, States N., Private, October 1, 1861.

Dieffenbacher, George, Private, October 25, 1861.

Dusing, Daniel D., Private, September 14, 1861.

Dusinger, Isaih D., Private, September 14, 1861.

Easton, Elisha, Private, September 14, 1861.

Fessler, Jonathan F., Private, September 14, 1861.

Flory, Barney, Private, September 14, 1861.

French, Teter, Private, October 1, 1861.

Frizzel, Dennis H., Private, October 1, 1861.

Fulton, David, Private, October 1, 1861.

Fultz, Frederick, Private, October 1, 1861.

Funury, Phillip, Private, October 1, 1861.

Gardener, Jeremiah, Private, October 1, 1861.

Green, Martin V. B., Private, September 14, 1861.

Grove John W., Private, October 1, 1861.

Hagerman, Martin L., Private, September 14, 1861.

Hemphill, Alexander, Private, September 14, 1861.

Hessong, Samuel W., Private, September 14, 1861.

Hoover, William H., Private, September 14, 1861.

House, Leonard D., Private, September 14, 1861.

Jones, George, Private, September 14, 1861.

Kile, Daniel, Private, September 14, 1861.

Law, James, Private, October 1, 1861.

Lawver, Elliott J., Private, October 1, 1861.

Lizer, John, Private, October 1, 1861.

Lopp, George, Private, September 14, 1861.

Marlow, Samuel, Private, October 1, 1861.

Marks, Benjamin, Private, September 14, 1861.

Martin, James, Private, September 14, 1861.

McCoy, Robert, Private, September 14, 1861.

McKinsey, Jacob, Private, September 14, 1861.

Mead, James, Private, October 12, 1861.

Miller, George, Private, September 14, 1861.

Mock, Godfrey, Private, September 14, 1861.

Norris, John, Private, September 14, 1861.

O'Sullivan, John Mc., Private, October 1, 1861.

Proctor, William H., Private, September 14, 1861.

Reese, Joseph E., Private, October 1, 1861.

Ridenour, Thomas, Private, October 1, 1861.

Robinson, Peter, Private, September 14, 1861.

Rohrback, William H., Private, September 14, 1861.

Rohrer, Daniel, Private, October 1, 1861.

Ryan, James, Private, October 1, 1861.

Shover, John D., Private, October 1, 1861.

Six, John T., Private, September 14, 1861.

Smith, William A., Private, October 1, 1861.

Stern, William H., Private, October 1, 1861.

Stouffer, Abraham, Private, October 1, 1861.

Swope, Michael, Private, September 14, 1861.

Tracey, Robert B., Private, October 1, 1861.

Waitz, Herman C., Private, October 1, 1861.

Walter, Simon, Private, September 14, 1861.

Ward, Josephus C., Private, September 14, 1861.

Weltz, George C., Private, September 14, 1861.

Witmer, David, Private, September 14, 1861.

Yeakle, Louis, Private, September 14, 1861.

Young, William H., Private, September 14, 1861.

Young, Zachariah, Private, October 1, 1861.

Zimmerman, Joseph, Private, September 14, 1861.

COMPANY F

Anderson, James R., Private, September 4, 1861.

Barger, Leander, Private, September 4, 1861.

Barthlow, John, Private, September 4, 1861.

Bayne, John, Private, September 4, 1861.

Blamer, Samuel, Private, September 4, 1861.

Bowles, John T., Private, September 4, 1861.

Bradshaw, George, Private, September 1, 1861.

Brill, George, Private, September 4, 1861.

Callahan, Phillip, Private, September 4, 1861.

Campbell, William, Private, September 4, 1861.

Chase, Samuel, Private, September 4, 1861.

Clark, John H., Private, September 4, 1861.

Connor, Patrick, Private, September 4, 1861.

Connor, Peter, Private, September 4, 1861.

Cosley, Thomas L., Private, September 4, 1861.

Dick, James, Private, September 4, 1861.

Eichelberger, Singleton, Private, September 4, 1861.

Ernst, George, Private, September 4, 1861.

Etzler, John H., Private, October 18, 1861.

Everitt, John H., Private, September 4, 1861.

Fink, Jacob, Private, September 4, 1861.

Forback, John, Private, September 22, 1861.

Foutz, George W., Private, September 4, 1861.

Frush, John D., Private, August 21, 1861.

Frush, Samuel, Private, September 4, 1861.

Greer, Robert W., Private, September 4, 1861.

Gyer, George O., Private, September 4, 1861.

Hafely, Joel, Private, September 4, 1861.

Hall, David, Private, September 4, 1861.

Hall, David D., Private, September 4, 1861.

Hall, John B., Private, September 4, 1861.

Hall, Joseph J., Private, September 4, 1861.

Hall, Levi M., Private, September 4, 1861.

Hardinger, Reuben, Private, September 4, 1861.

Harmison, Isaac, Private, September 4, 1861.

Hartman, David, Private, September 4, 1861.

Hoover, Samuel, Private, September 4, 1861.

Horner, John, Private, September 4, 1861.

Householder, John, Private, September 4, 1861.

Householder, George, Private, September 4, 1861.

Householder, Samuel, Private, September 4, 1861.

Hughes, Joseph L., Private, September 4, 1861.

Inglebright, Michael, Private, September 4, 1861.

Keplinger, Edward, Private, September 4, 1861.

Kinsel, Martin, Private, September 4, 1861.

Knepper, William D., Private, September 4, 1861.

Kreps, Benjamin F., Private, September 4, 1861.

Mannahan, Lewis, Private, September 4, 1861.

McAlister, Andrew J., Private, September 4, 1861.

McCarter, George, Private, September 4, 1861.

McCarthy, John, Private, September 4, 1861.

McLain, John D., Private, September 4, 1861.

Miller, George W., Private, September 4, 1861.

Miller, Washington, Private, September 4, 1861.

Murphy, Edward, Private, September 4, 1861.

Must, George, Private, September 4, 1861.

Nash, Ephraim, Private, September 4, 1861.

Null, James A., Private, September 4, 1861.

Null, Robert R., Private, September 4, 1861.

Pentaney, James, Private, September 4, 1861.

Pittinger, Abraham M., Private, September 4, 1861.

Plotner, Richard R., Private, September 4, 1861.

Plotner, Samuel, Private, September 4, 1861.

Potter, John T., Private, September 4, 1861.

Potter, William H., Private, September 4, 1861.

Prather, Isaac T., Private, September 4, 1861.

Purnell, Frederick, Private, September 4, 1861.

Purnell, James H., Private, September 4, 1861.

Small, Leander, Private, September 4, 1861.

Sowers, Jacob, Private, September 4, 1861.

Stokes, Samuel, Private, September 4, 1861.

Sosey, John N., Private, September 4, 1861.

Stoner, Franklin, Private, September 4, 1861.

Troupe, Joseph C., Corporal, September 4, 1861.

Tyson, Basil, Private, September 4, 1861.

Warner, Frederick G., Private, September 4, 1861.

Warner, Phillip, Private, September 4, 1861.

Westerhouse, John, Private, September 4, 1861.

Worley, Jonathan T., Private, September 4, 1861.

Young, William H., Private, September 4, 1861.

COMPANY G

Billingsly, William T., Private, October 24, 1861.

Bloom, David, Private, October 24, 1861.

Brady, John, Private, October 24, 1861.

Breighner, Samuel I., Private, October 24, 1861.

Bruner, Rufus, P., Private, October 24, 1861.

Buckman, Edward, Private, October 24, 1861.

Burns, David W., Private, December 11, 1861.

Cathell, Edward, Private, October 24, 1861.

Colley, John W., Private, October 24, 1861.

Colston, David, Private, October 24, 1861.

Conrey, Joseph D., Private, October 24, 1861.

Coppersmith, Joseph D., Private, October 24, 1861.

Cullison, Micajah M., Private, October 24, 1861.

Daugherty, James, Private, October 24, 1861.

Dennis, John, Private, October 24, 1861.

Dorsey, Francis, Private, October 28, 1861.

Eckard, Theodore, Private, October 24, 1861.

Elliot, John, Private, October 24, 1861.

England, William G., Private, October 24, 1861.

Engler, Herod P., Private, October 24, 1861.

Ervin, James, Private, October 24, 1861.

Fink, John, Private, October 24, 1861.

Fleagle, Uriah, Private, October 24, 1861.

Ford, Francis M., Private, October 24, 1861.

Ford, William H., Private, October 24, 1861.

Frizzle, Silas, Private, October 24, 1861.

Gatton, George W., Private, October 24, 1861.

Gill, Oliver E., Private, October 24, 1861.

Glass, John, Private, October 24, 1861.

Goodwin, George W., Private, October 24, 1861.

Grace, Henry, Private, October 24, 1861.

Green, Thomas, Private, October 24, 1861.

Haifley, Jacob S., Private, October 24, 1861.

Henrickson, Abraham, Private, October 24, 1861.

Hershberger, John J., Private, October 24, 1861.

Hoffman, Daniel, Private, December 10, 1861.

Jackson, Jonathan R., Private, August 24, 1861.

Kinsey, Joseph A., Private, October 24, 1861.

Kuhn, George F., Private, October 24, 1861.

Lowe, Caleb B., Private, October 24, 1861.

Lowery, Matthew J., Private, October 24, 1861.

Manyhan, Patrick, Private, October 24, 1861.

Martin, John, Private, October 24, 1861.

Martin, Warren T., Private, October 24, 1861.

Mathias, Cornelius, Private, October 24, 1861.

Mathias, Sylvester, Private, October 24, 1861.

McGee, Levi, Private, October 24, 1861.

McKinsey, Thomas, Private, October 24, 1861.

McMackin, Andrew J., Private, October 24, 1861.

Miller, John, Private, October 24, 1861.

Miller, Peter, Private, October 24, 1861.

Miller, Peter L., Private, October 24, 1861.

Miller, Samuel, Private, October 24, 1861.

Mitchell, Henry T., Private, October 24, 1861.

Morris, Charles H., Private, October 24, 1861.

Myers, Anthony, Private, October 24, 1861.

Myres, George R., Private, October 24, 1861.

Nafe, Henry, Private, October 24, 1861.

Parker, Augustus M., Private, October 24, 1861.

Pierce, Richard, Private, October 24, 1861.

Roberts, William A., Private, November 20, 1861.

Sefford, Sebastian, Private, October 24, 1861.

Shriner, Alfred, Private, October 24, 1861.

Sipe, John A., Private, December 10, 1861.

Stonesifer, Ephraim, Private, October 24, 1861.

Stonesifer, Jacob D., Private, October 24, 1861.

Sullivan, Abraham C., Private, October 24, 1861.

Sweetman, Robert, Private, October 24, 1861.

Trippe, Nicholas H., Private, October 24, 1861.

Unwin, William, Private, October 24, 1861.

Wetherell, James O., Private, October 24, 1861.

Williams, George W., Private, October 24, 1861.

Wheeler, John J., Private, October 24, 1861.

Wooddy, James R., Private, October 24, 1861.

Yellott, Charles M., Sergeant, October 24, 1861.

Yingling, Aaron, Private, October 24, 1861.

COMPANY H

Bamford, William S., Private, September 14, 1861.

Beck, John J., Private, October 25, 1861.

Bender, George, Private, October 25, 1861.

Bender, William, Private, October 25, 1861.

Benner, Aaron B., Private, October 25, 1861.

Best, Asher, Private, October 25, 1861.

Bingham, Oliver, Private, October 25, 1861.

Bird, William, private, October 25, 1861.

Blakeney, John, Private, October 25, 1861.

Boyd, James, Private, September 14, 1861.

Butler, James, Private, October 25, 1861.

Carns, John, Private, October 25, 1861.

Caswell, Andrew, Private, September 14, 1861.

Caswell, Andrew, private, September 14, 1861.

Clagett, John T., Private, September 14, 1861.

Cline, James, Private, October 25, 1861.

Connor, Gilbert W., Private, October 25, 1861.

Cox, Joseph, Private, October 25, 1861.

Cramer, James, Private, October 25, 1861.

Cuddy, John, Private, October 25, 1861.

Cunningham, Edward, Private, October 25, 1861.

Cunningham, James, Private, October 25, 1861.

Davis, James, Private, October 25, 1861.

Delanney, Benjamin F., Private, September 14, 1861.

Dell, Rufus M., Private, November 4, 1861.

Diggs, Isaac M., Private, October 25, 1861.

Dillow, Thomas A., Private, October 25, 1861.

Dye, John W., Private, October 25, 1861.

Glass, Martin, Private, September 14, 1861.

Greenwalt, Abraham, Private, September 14, 1861.

Grim, Josiah C., Private, October 25, 1861.

Grimm, Eli R., Private, September 14, 1861.

Hanes, George W., Private, October 25, 1861.

Hanes, Henry R., Private, September 14, 1861.

Hanes, Jeremiah, Private, September 14, 1861.

Holtz, Robert T., Private, October 25, 1861.

Houser, Aaron, Private, October 25, 1861.

Keyser, Charles R., Private, October 25, 1861.

Mann, John S., Private, October 25, 1861.

Marrow, Andrew J., Private, September 14, 1861.

Marrow, James, Private, September 14, 1861.

Marrow, John, Private, September 14, 1861.

Marmaduke, Reuben, Private, October 25, 1861.

McCoy, Joseph, Private, September 14, 1861.

McCoy, Henry, Private, September 14, 1861.

McDonald, Robert E., Private, October 25, 1861.

McGregor, George S., Private, October 25, 1861.

McKernan, Thomas, Private, October 25, 1861.

McManus, Peter, Private, September 14, 1861.

Misinger, John, Private, October 25, 1861.

Monegan, Jeremiah, Private, December 13, 1861.

Mongan, Hezekiah, Private, October 25, 1861.

Morrisy, John, Private, September 14, 1861.

Myres, John F., Private, September 14, 1861.

Myres, Samuel, Private, September 14, 1861.

Nicholson, Joshua W., Private, October 25, 1861.

Norris, John W., Private, October 25, 1861.

Nuse, Peter, Private, October 25, 1861.

Palmer, William M., Private, October 25, 1861.

Pitzer, Joseph H., Private, October 25, 1861.

Poffenbarger, John R., Private, September 14, 1861.

Railey, John S., Private, August 15, 1861.

Renner, Leander, Private, August 15, 1861.

Rhodrick, Augustus A., Private, October 25, 1861.

Santman, George W., Private, September 14, 1861.

Santman, James, Private, December 3, 1861.

Seiss, Hiram S., Private, September 14, 1861.

Sharer, John W., Private, October 25, 1861.

Sharer, William, Private, October 25, 1861.

Shoemaker, William, Private, October 25, 1861.

Smith, Joseph E., Private, September 14, 1861.

Staubs, Josiah F., Private, October 25, 1861.

Staubs, William H., Private, October 25, 1861.

Stevens, Benjamin, Private, October 25, 1861.

Stoner, William, Private, October 25,1861.

Swain, James F., Private, October 25, 1861.

Ward, James H., Private, October 25, 1861.

Wilhelm, Jacob, Private, October 25, 1861.

Willitt, John W., Private, October 25, 1861.

COMPANY I

Abbott, Edward G., Private, September 14, 1861.

Ashton, John H., Private, November 30, 1861.

Bable, John C., Private, November 30, 1861.

Bailey, George W., Private, November 30, 1861.

Bast, George M. D., Private, November 30, 1861.

Baylis, Joseph, Private, November 30, 1861.

Betson, Joseph T., Private, December 13, 1861.

Bingham, Isaac N., Private, November 30, 1861.

Bitzenberger, Abraham, Private, November 30, 1861.

Bowers, John, Private, November 30, 1861.

Brown, Francis L., Private, November 30, 1861.

Brown, Jefferson, Private, November 30, 1861.

Buck, Silas, Private, November 30, 1861.

Burk, William, Private, November 30, 1861.

Burk, William H., Private, November 30, 1861.

Carlin, Francis T., Private, November 30, 1861.

Carnes, David L., Private, November 30, 1861.

Castle, John, Private, October 1, 1861.

Clopper, John A., Private, October 1, 1861.

Craman, Joseph, Private, November 30, 1861.

Derr, Ely, Private, November 30, 1861.

Derr, George F., Private, November 30, 1861.

Derr, John, Private, November 30, 1861.

Dillon, George B., Private, November 30, 1861.

Dillon, William, Private, November 30, 1861.

Dunlop, James, Private, November 30, 1861.

Eader, Peter M., Private, November 30, 1861.

Feezer, James H. E., Private, November 30, 1861.

Gardner, John P., Private, November 30, 1861.

Getzendanner, Solomon J., Private, November 30, 1861.

Gilbert, John, Private, November 30, 1861.

Gormley, Mathew, Private, November 30, 1861.

Gouff, John, Private, September 14, 1861.

Harman, Geroge H., Private, November 30, 1861.

Hartzock, David, Private, November 30, 1861.

Hassett, John, Private, November 30, 1861.

Jacobs, Thomas, Private, September 14, 1861.

Jennings, John W., Private, November 30, 1861.

Kane, John T., Private, November 30, 1861.

Kauffman, Jonathan F., Private, November 30, 1861.

Keefer, Christian, Private, November 30, 1861.

Keyser, Eugene, Private, November 30, 1861.

Kline, William H., Private, November 30, 1861.

Koontz, Elias, Private, November 30, 1861.

Koontz, James, Private, November 30, 1861.

Lambert, George D., Private, November 30, 1861.

Lambert, William H., Private, November 30, 1861.

Main, Enos C., Private, November 30, 1861.

Main, Jacob I., Private, November 30, 1861.

McCoy, Aaron, Private, September 14, 1861.

Mehrling, August, Private, November 30, 1861.

Mehrling, Conradt, Private, November 30, 1861.

Mehrling, Henry, Private, November 30, 1861.

Miller, Warner, Private, November 30, 1861.

Misner, George W., Private, December 17, 1861.

Moore, Jacob M., Private, November 30, 1861.

Muck, George F., Private, November 30, 1861.

Pendergast, John, Private, November 30, 1861.

Phoebus, Charles E., Private, November 30, 1861.

Porter, Gassaway, Private, November 30, 1861.

Ports, David E., Private, November 30, 1861.

Renner, Peter, Private, November 30, 1861.

Rohrer, Leonidas T., Private, September 14, 1861.

Rohrer, William H. H., Private, November 30, 1861.

Seaman, Lewis W., Private, November 30, 1861.

Shelton, Thomas, Private, November 30, 1861.

Shook, Lewis A., Private, November 30, 1861.

Shope, Charles B., Private, November 30, 1861.

Shope, Milton W. W., Private, November 30, 1861.

Shuffer, Jonathan W., Private, November 30, 1861.

Smith, George C., Private, December 17, 1861.

Smith, Henry F., Private, November 30, 1861.

Stedding, Henry, Private, November 30, 1861.

Steel, George W., Private, November 30, 1861.

Toms, George W., Private, November 30, 1861.

Wachter, Elijah R., Private, November 30, 1861.

Watson, Jonathan W., Private, November 30, 1861.

Webster, Daniel F., Private, December 23, 1861.

White, John J., Private, November 30, 1861.

Zumbrum, Thomas E., Private, November 30, 1861.

COMPANY K

Abbott, Robert J., Private, December 13, 1861.

Abbott, John, Private, December 13, 1861.

Allender, John, Private, December 13, 1861.

Attick, Conrad, Private, December 13, 1861.

Auzengruber, Mathias, Private, December 13, 1861.

Barnhouse, Christian F. T., Private, December 13, 1861.

Bayne, William C., Private, December 13, 1861.

Bellison, Milton, Private, December 13, 1861.

Benner, Thomas N., Private, December 13, 1861.

Best, Nathaniel, Private, December 13, 1861.

Bond, Battle, Private, December 13, 1861.

Brown, Franklin, Private, December 13, 1861.

Brown, James E., Private, December 13, 1861.

Bruce, Jonathan H. R., Private, December 13, 1861.

Brummel, Joseph, Private, December 13, 1861.

Burger, John, Private, December 13, 1861.

Calp, John L., Private, December 13, 1861.

Claypoole, George W., Private, December 13, 1861.

Colbert, Samuel, Private, December 13, 1861.

Collins, Thomas P., Private, December 13, 1861.

Cook, William, Private, December 13, 1861.

Coulson, Jonathan B., Private, December 13, 1861.

Crabb, Jeremiah, Private, December 13, 1861.

Craft, John, Private, December 13, 1861.

Davis, Edward, Private, December 13, 1861.

Donegan, Owen, Private, December 13, 1861.

Dorsey, Daniel, Private, December 13, 1861.

Essender, Charles, Private, December 13, 1861.

Fisher, James, Private, December 13, 1861.

Frank, George, Private, December 13, 1861.

Freshman, John, Private, December 13, 1861.

Gill, Robert N., Private, December 13, 1861.

Grimes, John T., Private, December 13, 1861.

Haddel. William, Private, December 13, 1861.

Hagan, James, Private, December 13, 1861.

Hahn, Michael J., Private, December 13, 1861.

Haines, Andrew, Private, December 13, 1861.

Hancock, William, Private, December 13, 1861.

Harris, William H., Private, December 13, 1861.

House, Martin V., Private, December 13, 1861.

Huggins, James E., Private, December 13, 1861.

Ingels, Alexander, Private, December 13, 1861.

Labadie, Joseph E., Private, September 14, 1861.

Lambert, Jessie B., Private, December 21, 1861.

Lowry, George G., Private, December 27, 1861.

Luts, Frederick, Private, December 14, 1861.

Maloney, Joseph, Private, October 24, 1861.

Manly, Michael, Private, December 13, 1861.

Mann, Charles, Private, December 13, 1861.

Martin, William T., Private, December 13, 1861.

McCombs, William, Private, October 24, 1861.

McDonald, Lawrence, Private, December 13, 1861.

Menter, Uriah, Private, December 13, 1861.

Miller, William T., Private, December 13, 1861.

Mules, David H., Private, October 25, 1861.

Neibergall, Lewis W., Private, December 13, 1861.

Poole, William H., Private, December 13, 1861.

Ray, John M., Private, December 13, 1861.

Roop, George W., Private, October 25, 1861.

Roop, John W., Private, October 25, 1861.

Roop, William H., Private, December 13, 1861.

Saunders, William F., Private, December 13, 1861.

Schmidt, Francis, Private, December 13, 1861.

Selb, Valentine, Private, December 13, 1861.

Severns, Nicholas, Private, December 13, 1861.

Shuff, Thomas. Private, December 13, 1861.

Shuff, William, Private, December 13, 1861.

Sittig, Augustus, Private, December 13, 1861.

Squire, Thruston E., Private, December 13, 1861.

Stahl, Ezra, Private, December 13, 1861.

Stevens, Henry, Private, December 13, 1861.

Stoffer, Simson, Private, December 13, 1861.

Thompson, William A., Private, December 13, 1861.

Tool, Patrick, Private, December 13, 1861.

Welsh, John H., Private, December 13, 1861.

Wilhelm, Henry B., Private, December 13, 1861.

FIRST REGIMENT
POTOMAC HOME BRIGADE CAVALRY
"COLES CAVALRY"

COMPANY A

Albaugh, Basil H., 1st Sergeant, August 10, 1861.

Apple, Julius C., Corporal, August 10, 1861.

Asherman, William, Private, August 10, 1861.

Bable, Christian, Private, August 10, 1861.

Barrack, Prestley I., Private, August 10, 1861.*

Barthelow, John H., Private, August 20, 1861.**

Beatty, Charles W., Farrier, August 10, 1861.

Bechtol, John W., Private, August 10, 1861.

Beeler, John C., Corporal, August 10, 1861.

Belding, Samuel P., Private, August 10, 1861.

Betson, Joseph, Private, December 1, 1861.

Bishop, Charles A., Sergeant, August 10, 1861.

Brogunier, James, Private, August 10, 1861.

Burk, John, Bugler, August 10, 1861.

Carnes, David W., Teamster, August 10, 1861.

Caughlin, Peter J., Private, August 10, 1861.

Cline, Frederick, Private, August 10, 1861.

Cline, Warren, Private, August 10, 1861.

Corbey, William, Private, August 10, 1861.

Crim, John W., Farrier, August 10, 1861.

Crist, Henry, Private, August 10, 1861.

Crum, William D., Teamster, August 10, 1861.

Crutchley, Milton C., Private, August 10, 1861.*

Cyrus, Richard H., Private, August 10, 1861.

Cyrus, William D., Corporal, August 10, 1861.

Dellett, John J., Private, August 10, 1861.

Dern, Abraham, Private, August 10, 1861.

Devilbiss, Charles V., Private, August 10, 1861.

Devilbiss, Isaac T., Sergeant, August 10, 1861.

Dixon, Franklin A., Private, August 10, 1861.

Ealey, James, Private, August 10, 1861.*

Etchison, John F. P., Private, August 10, 1861.*

Esworthy, Nathaniel, Corporal, August 10, 1861.

Firestone, Martin L., Corporal, August 10, 1861.

Fogle, Solomon, Private, August 10, 1861.

Fouch, Temple, Private, August 10, 1861.

Fraily, John F., Private, August 10, 1861.

Gannon, Edward V., Sergeant, August 10, 1861.

Gant, John F., Private, August 10, 1861.

Grams, Jonathan C., Corporal, August 10, 1861.

Green, Henson T. C., Sergeant, August 10, 1861.

Hall, David D., Private, August 1, 1861.

Hall, Joseph J., 1st Sergeant, August 1, 1861.

Hall, Levi M., Corporal, August 21, 1861.

Hargett, David Z., Private, August 21, 1861.

Harris, Edward V., Private, November 5, 1861.

Hartsock, Jonathan T., Private, August 10, 1861.

Hildebrand, John T., Private, August 10, 1861.

Houck, David E., Private, August 10, 1861.

Hudson, John A., Sergeant, August 10, 1861.

Kauffman, Martin L., Q. M. Sergeant, August 10, 1861.

Keedy, Walter H., Private, August 10, 1861.

Kelly, John A., Private, August 10, 1861.

Kintz, Daniel, Bugler, August 10, 1861.

Koontz, James H., Private, August 10, 1861.

Lacoy, Alfred, Private, August 11, 1861.

Lease, George W., Q. M. Sergeant, August 10, 1861.

Lewis, William H., Private, August 10, 1861.

Link, Daniel, Sergeant, August 10, 1861.

Link, George, Private, August 10, 1861.

Main, Cornelius, Private, August 10, 1861.**

Main, Joseph D., Private, August 10, 1861.

Mathews, Cormenius, Corporal, August 10, 1861.

McDevitt, James H., Corporal, August 10, 1861.

McKnight, James T., Com. Sergeant, August 10, 1861.

McMan, Thomas, Private, August 10, 1861.

Miller, Henry, Private, August 10, 1861.

Orrison, Logan, 1st Sergeant, August 10, 1861.

Poole, William H., Corporal, August 10, 1861.

Rice, Job, 1st Sergeant, August 10, 1861.

Silver, George W., Private, August 10, 1861.**

Soper, Franklin S., Corporal, August 10, 1861.

Staley, Simon M., Private, August 10, 1861.

Stone, Edward V., Private, August 10, 1861.

Stone, Samuel, Private, August 10, 1861.

Stott, James H., Private, August 10, 1861.

Stottlemyer, Andrew J., Private, August 10, 1861.

Stull, Dennis, Private, August 10, 1861.

Tall, Erasmus, Corporal, August 10, 1861.

Tinterman, William, Private, August 10, 1861.

Tolinger, George, Private, August 10, 1861.

Ullrich, William F., Sergeant, August 10, 1861.

Virts, James M. W., Sergeant, August 10, 1861.

Wachter, Calvin S., Private, August 10, 1861.

Wachter, Gideon R., Private, August 10, 1861.

Wachter, Thomas M., Corporal, August 10, 1861.

Washburn, David L., Corporal, August 10, 1861.

West, Jonathan W. B., Corporal, August 10, 1861.

Wheeler, Thomas, Sergeant, August 10, 1861.

Yates, Charles M., Sergeant, August 10, 1861.

Yeakle, Henry W., Private, August 10, 1861.

Zimmerman, Lewis M., Sergeant, August 10, 1861.

*Transferred to Company I, First Regiment, Potomac Home Brigade Infantry.

**Transferred to Company F, First Regiment, Potomac Home Brigade Infantry.

COMPANY B

Anderson, Jacob, Private, August 24, 1861.

Anderson, Robert, Private, August 24, 1861.

Baltz, John, Private, August 24, 1861.

Bell, Phillip M., Sergeant, August 24, 1861.

Berndt, Charles F. O., Private, August 27, 1861.

Boggs, Harrison, Corporal, September 4, 1861.

Boner, John H., Corporal, August 24, 1861.

Breish, Jacob F., Private, August 24, 1861.

Butts, William H. H., Private, August 24, 1861.

Cakerice, Michael, Private, August 24, 1861.

Carpenter, Jonathan, Private, August 27, 1861.

Dennis, Jeremiah, Private, September 4, 1861.

Diehl, Reuben P., Private, August 24, 1861.

Dick, David, Sergeant, September 4, 1861.

Dougherty, Benjamin L., Private, August 24, 1861.

Drake, Vinton, Private, August 30, 1861.

Elms, Robert, Private, August 24, 1861.

Every, Abraham, Private, August 30, 1861.

Eyre, Isaac P., Private, September 2, 1861.

Filler, Benjamin F., Corporal, November 12, 1861.

Fink, Michael, Private, September 3, 1861.

Fuss, Gotlieb, Private, August 24, 1861.

Gletner, James D., Bugler, September 4, 1861.

Goodman, John, Farrier, August 30, 1861.

Graybill, Henry, Private, August 28, 1861.

Heisner, George W., Private, September 1, 1861.

High, David B., Farrier, August 24, 1861.

Hoeflich, Jonathan F., Saddler, September 4, 1861.

Holland, Daniel R., Private, August 24, 1861.

Holland, Joseph L., Corporal, August 24, 1861.

Jack, John C., Private, September 3, 1861.

Jack, Mathias W., Sergeant, August 24, 1861.

Jackson, John, Private, August 24, 1861.

Johnson, William, Sergeant, September 4, 1861.

Kerlin, Daniel, Private, September 1, 1861.

Kerns, John J., Sergeant, August 24, 1861.

Kershner, Andrew J., 1st Sergeant, August 24, 1861.

Kershner, Joseph H., Private, August 24, 1861.

Kime, Ephraim H., Private, September 3, 1861.

Koppisch, Charles E. H., Corporal, August 4, 1861.

Kraft, Andrew, Private, August 30, 1861.

Kretzer, George, Private, September 4, 1861.

Lincks, Henry, Sergeant, September 4, 1861.

Litton, Anthony, Corporal, September 4, 1861.

Lowman, George W., Corporal, September 4, 1861.

Loy, Isaiah F., Corporal, September 2, 1861.

Martin, Charles A., Saddle Sergeant, September 4, 1861.

Mayhew, Harvey, Private, September 2, 1861.

McAtee, Benjamin F., Private, August 24, 1861.

McAtee, Thomas, Private, August 24, 1861.

McKinney, Joseph L., Private, September 2, 1861.

McLucas, William, Corporal, September 10, 1861.

Metcalf, Thomas O., Q. M. Sergeant, August 24, 1861.

Miller, Daniel, Private, September 2, 1861.

Miller, John A., Private, September 4, 1861.

Miller, Joseph, Private, September 4, 1861.

Moore, James D., Private, September 3, 1861.

Munson, Jonathan J., Wagoner, August 24, 1861.

Myers, John W., Corporal, August 24, 1861.

Myers, Walter S., Private, August 24, 1861.

Nicewarner, Isaiah, Private, August 29, 1861.

Newcomer, John, Private, October 7, 1861.

Perrell, Reason, Sergeant, August 24, 1861.

Ragor, James W., Private, September 2, 1861.

Rine, E. H., Private, August 24, 1861.

Riser, William, Private, August 24, 1861.

Rivers, Samuel, Farrier, August 30, 1861.

Robinett, Mathias, Corporal, November 12, 1861.

Rockwell, Jonathan H., Private, August 24, 1861.

Rotorff, David P., Private, September 4, 1861.

Scleigh, Charles A., Bugler, September 4, 1861.

Shadrach, Lancelot M., Private, August 24, 1861.

Smith, Adolphus W., Corporal, September 4, 1861.

Smith, Harrison, Private, August 24, 1861.

Smith, John W., Private, September 3, 1861.

Smith, Lewis C., Private, August 30, 1861.

Socey, Abraham L., Bugler, September 2, 1861.

Sofficool, Joseph W., Private, August 24, 1861.

Sofficool, William S., Private, August 21, 1861.

Spitznas, Christian, Private, August 24, 1861.

Stephny, William H., Corporal, August 4, 1861.

Stine, William F., Corporal, October 17, 1861.

Stottlemeyer, Andrew J., Private, September 1, 1861.

Stouffer, Jacob C., 1st Sergeant, August 24, 1861.

Strode, Daniel, Private, September 1, 1861.

Strode, S. R. T., Private, September 1, 1861.

Tingstrom, William, Private, August 24, 1861.

Turner, Adam, Private, August 24, 1861.

Weaver, George, Private, August 24, 1861.

Weaver, William H., Private, October 30, 1861.

Wentz, William, Private, September 4, 1861.

Wolf, David H., Private, September 3, 1861.

Wolf, Hamilton, Private, August 24, 1861.

Wright, William, Private, September 4, 1861.

COMPANY C

Annan, Andrew A., Sergeant, August 27, 1861.

Bennet, Joseph A., Wagoner, September 4, 1861.

Boller, John A., Private, August 27, 1861.

Bostick, Samuel R., Com. Sergeant, October 19, 1861.

Cease, George, Private, September 4, 1861.

Coble, Maxwell J., 1st Bugler, September 1, 1861.

Coyle, William A., Private, September 4, 1861.

Crooks, Robert E., Private, November 21, 1861.

Crouse, William A., Private, August 27, 1861.

Currens, William N., Sergeant, August 27, 1861.

Diehl, Martin, Q. M. Sergeant, August 27, 1861.

Dorsey, Charles F., Teamster, August 31, 1861.

Duphon, Thomas W., Private, August 27, 1861.

Flohr, Reuben A., Private, September 4, 1861.

Fites, Theodore, Private, September 3, 1861.

Fritchey, Alfred N., Private, September 3, 1861.

Gelwicks, George T., Corporal, August 27, 1861.

Gettier, Henry, Private, September 6, 1861.

Gettier, John F., Private, August 27, 1861.

Gillelan, George L., Private, August 27, 1861.

Gilson, Charles A., Corporal, August 27, 1861.

Gilson, John E., Sergeant, August 27, 1861.

Grimes, James, Private, August 27, 1861.

Gwinn, George W., Sergeant, August 27, 1861.

Hartzel, Jacob, Private, August 27, 1861.

Hilleary, Henry C., Corporal, September 10, 1861.

Hizer, Louis, Private, September 12, 1861.

242

Hollebaugh, John Z., Private, August 27, 1861.

Huber, John M., Private, September 4, 1861.

Hughes, Henry, Private, August 27, 1861.

Johnson, Oliver, Corporal, August 27, 1861.

Kehn, Calvin D., Private, September 3, 1861.

King, Hiram, Private, September 5, 1861.

Knott, John E., Private, August 27, 1861.

Longwell, David W., 1st Sergeant, August 27, 1861.

Lott, William H., Private, August 27, 1861.

McAllister, Theodore, Sergeant, August 27, 1861.

McFarland, William J., Private, September 19, 1861.

McCullough, James, Private, August 27, 1861.

Merring, Edward W., Private, September 3, 1861.

Morrison, Lake B., Private, August 27, 1861.

Morritz, John M., Private, August 31, 1861.

Plowman, Mosheim S., Corporal, August 27, 1861.

Reaver, Henry A., Corporal, September 17, 1861.

Reck, Elias O., Private, September 3, 1861.

Richards, Isaac, Private, August 27, 1861.

Scott, James A., Corporal, August 27, 1861.

Shaugheny, John, Private, August 28, 1861.

Sherfey, Thomas R., Bugler, September 2, 1861.

Shilt, David, Private, August 28, 1861.

Shriver, George W., Sergeant, August 27, 1861.

Sites, John C., Corporal, August 27, 1861.

Spangler, George, Private, August 27, 1861.

Sponcler, George D., Corporal, August 27, 1861.

Stahl, Jesse, Private, August 27, 1861.

Swann, John W., Corporal, August 27, 1861.

Test, Joseph U., Sergeant, September 4, 1861.

Thomas, Lewis E., Private, September 4, 1861.

Turle, Henry, Private, September 4, 1861.

Walker, A. M., Q. M. Sergeant, August 27, 1861.

Weigle, Daniel E., Private, August 27, 1861.

Weikert, George W., Private, August 27, 1861.

Weikert, William F., Farrier, August 27, 1861.

Welch, Oliver, Private, August 27, 1861.

Wenk, William B., Farrier, August 27, 1861.

White, William, Corporal, August 27, 1861.

Wible, Joseph E., Private, August 27, 1861.

Williar, George B., Farrier, November 21, 1861.

Wills, Joseph H. C., Corporal, August 27, 1861.

Wilson, Samuel D., Private, August 27, 1861.

Wolf, John F., Private, September 6, 1861.

Wolf, Peter, Private, September 6, 1861.

Wolf, Samuel J., Sergeant, August 27, 1861.

Wolford, Thomas, Private, August 27, 1861.

COMPANY D

Armstrong, Benjamin, Private, August 28, 1861.

Ault, Conrad, Private, November 27, 1861.

Ball, Charles E., Private, September 8, 1861.

Ball, Joseph N., Private, September 8, 1861.

Bennett, Andrew, Corporal, September 4, 1861.

Bowman, William H., Corporal, November 12, 1861.

Boyd, Andrew J., Private, August 28, 1861.

Brown, George D., Private, August 28, 1861.

Brown, Theophilus, Private, August 28, 1861.

Brown, Thomas, Private, August 28, 1861.

Bryan, Stephen, Sergeant, September 4, 1861.

Burford, George, Private, September 4, 1861.

Casey, James, Farrier, November 27, 1861.

Chambers, Jonathan W., Private, November 16, 1861.

Cox, George H., Private, November 27, 1861.

Craig, Donald, Private, September 8, 1861.

Cross, Reason, Bugler, November 26, 1861.

Crutchley, Jonathan T., Private, November 23, 1861.

Davis, Charles F., Saddler, August 28, 1861.

Davis, George H., Bugler, July 28, 1861.

Davis, Lafayette, Private, November 23, 1861.

Dawson, Lewis, Private, November 10, 1861.

Eddy, John H., Private, September 14, 1861.

Edmonds, Esom, Private, October 14, 1861.

Eltenhead, Thomas D., Private, November 9, 1861.

Ernshaw, James N., Private, November 10, 1861.

Evans, James D., Private, September 28, 1861.

Finnegan, Frank, Private, August 19, 1861.

Forwood, Samuel D., Private, September 4, 1861.

Fowler, Randolph, Private, November 9, 1861.

Frost, John, Private, September 4, 1861.

George, Stephen, Sergeant, August 28, 1861.

Gibbons, Oliver, Private, September 4, 1861.

Godfrey, Thomas, Private, August 28, 1861.

Goff, John J., Corporal, August 31, 1861.

Grogg, William H., Private, November 15, 1861.

Grubb, James W., Bugler, September 4, 1861.

Grubert, Charles, Private, November 27, 1861.

Hays, Edward A., Private, September 8, 1861.

Hillary, Edward, Private, November 27, 1861.

Hitzelberger, William J., Private, August 28, 1861.

Hofnagle, Charles, Private, November 9, 1861.

Howard, Henry, Saddler, November 7, 1861.

Hugg, Benjamin F., Private, November 27, 1861.

Iseminger, A., Private, November 7, 1861.

Kraft, John, Private, August 31, 1861.

Lewis, Arthur, Private, September 4, 1861.

Marks, Henry, Private, November 15, 1861.

McCauley, Adolphus, Private, November 27, 1861.

McConnell, Duncan, Private, August 28, 1861.

McCregor, William, Private, November 9, 1861.

Millholland, William, Private, August 28, 1861.

Mills, Amos A., Private, November 27, 1861.

Morris, Hickman M., Q. M. Sergeant, Nov. 27, 1861.

Newcomer, Christopher, Private, August 28, 1861.

Newcomer, David W., Private, November 9, 1861.

O'Brian, John, Private, August 31, 1861.

Orr, James C., Private, August 31, 1861.

Padgett, Jonathan W., Private, November 9, 1861.

Pierce, John Q., Private, September 7, 1861.

Purden, Charles B., Private, August 28, 1861.

Rhodes, Augustus C., Sergeant, October 7, 1861.

Sakers, John S., Corporal, September 4, 1861.

Seifert, John, Private, August 28, 1861.

Shank, Otho H., Sergeant, November 27, 1861.

Simons, John, Private, November 15, 1861.

Smith, William H., Corporal, September 4, 1861.

Stayton, William F., Private, August 31, 1861.

Stansbury, Alpheus, Sergeant, September 16, 1861.

Stansbury, John W., Corporal, November 15, 1861.

Stuart, William H., Private, November 27, 1861.

Stull, George E., Private, November 15, 1861.

Sullivan, Jonathan W., Private, November 15, 1861.

Switzer, Jeremiah, Private, September 17, 1861.

Talbot, Joseph H., Private, August 31, 1861.

Trich, Henry C., Private, November 13, 1861.

Welch, Richard E., Private, November 11, 1861.

Welch, William H., Corporal, September 4, 1861.

Wheeling, George W., Private, November 11, 1861.

Williams, Jonathan L., Farrier, November 9, 1861.

Winter, Harvey G., Private, November 27, 1861.

Winters, Warren, Private, November 27, 1861.

Winters, William S., Private, November 15, 1861.

SECOND REGIMENT
POTOMAC HOME BRIGADE

COMPANY A

Cook, George, Corporal, August 27, 1861.

Cross, Henry, Private, August 27, 1861.

Durbin, George W., Private, August 27, 1861.

Ellenberger, Michael E., Private, August 24, 1861.

Gerloch, Anthony, Private, November 13, 1861.

Gouden, Louis N., Sergeant, August 24, 1861.

Kegg, Levi R., Private, October 29, 1861.

Kimberly, Hiram, Private, August 27, 1861.

Middleton, Benjamin, Corporal, August 27, 1861.

Mull, Andrew, Private, August 27, 1861.

Poole, Arthur A., Private, October 31, 1861.

Shupe, John, Private, August 27, 1861.

Snyder, Godfrey G., Musician, August 27, 1861.

White, Joseph, Corporal, August 27, 1861.

Whitmire, Nathan C., Corporal, August 27, 1861.

This company was raised to its full complement through the transfer of men from companies which were over-full. The Companies which contributed the bulk of the members of Company A were E, F, G, and H.

COMPANY B

Boyd, Lorenzo D., Private, August 27, 1861.

Crabtree, Martin, Private, August 27, 1861.

Darkey, Francis, Corporal, August 27, 1861.

Dowden, William, Musician, December 16, 1861.

Gorden, James, Private, December 1, 1861.

Gurtler, Frederick H., Private, August 12, 1861.

Helgoth, Jonathan H., Private, August 27, 1861.

Jackson, William W., Private, August 27, 1861.

McAtee, John D., Corporal, August 27, 1861.

McCall, Philander V., Private, August 27, 1861.

McCall, Jasper H., Private, August 27, 1861.

Miller, George W., Private, August 27, 1861

Reckley. Charles D., Private, August 27, 1861.

Reinick, John, Private, August 27, 1861.

Riley, Edward, Private, October 31, 1861.

Robey, Emanuel M., Private, August 27, 1861.

Ryan, David H., Private, August 27, 1861.

Spring, Apollos, Private, August 27, 1861.

Twigg, Charles, Private, August 27, 1861.

Twigg, Francis T., Private, August 27, 1861.

Weaver, George W., Corporal, September 24, 1861.

Weston, George W., Private, August 27, 1861.

Whittaker, Jordan, Private, December 16, 1861.

COMPANY C

Anthony, William, Private, August 1, 1861.

Auston, William, Musician, September 18, 1861.

Barnett, Joseph, Private, August 1, 1861.

Brady, John, Private, August 20, 1861.

Cole, Valentine, Private, August 27, 1861.

Cook, George, Private, September 2, 1861.

Cook, Henry, Private, September 15, 1861.

Croston, John W., Corporal, November 21, 1861.

Graham, Thomas, Private, August 28, 1861.

Halbert, John D., Private, December 18, 1861.

Kenny, Michael, Private, August 27, 1861.

Kight, Lewis F., Private, August 1, 1861.

Lannon, Patrick, Private, August 27, 1861.

Lyons, John, Private, August 27, 1861.

Michael, Henry H., Private, September 6, 1861.

Miller, Gilead, Corporal, August 27, 1861.

Miller, Kelita, Private, August, 27, 1861.

Miller, Thomas, Private, August 27, 1861.

Myers, Henry, Private, August 1, 1861.

Sigler, Thomas W., Corporal, November 1, 1861.

Swanger, Jonathan B., Private, August 27, 1861.

Wigfield, Elijah, Corporal, August 27, 1861.

Company D was not formed until 1865, and therefore is not included.

COMPANY E

Bacon, William I., Private, August 27, 1861.

Barkdoll, Jacob H., Private, August 27, 1861.*

Bise, William, Private, August 27, 1861.*

Boor, George W., Private, August 27, 1861.

Bray, Thomas, Private, August 27, 1861.

Brunner, Israel P., Private, August 27, 1861.

Brunner, William T., Private, August 27, 1861.

Cahill, John, Private, September 6, 1861.

Cessna, John, Private, August 27, 1861.

Cisel, Richard Z., Private, August 27, 1861.

Cisel, William H., Private, August 27, 1861.

Clise, Edward E., Private, August 27, 1861.

Couter, Robert S., Private, August 27, 1861.

Craggs, Jonathan B., September 20, 1861.

Daddysman, Edward A., Private, August 27, 1861.

Daddysman, George H., Private, August 27, 1861.*

Davis, Neri S., Private, August 27, 1861.

Deetz, William T., Private, August 27, 1861.

Degnan, John, Private, August 27, 1861.

Dowden, Lloyd H., Private, August 27, 1861.

Dunka, Martin, Private, August 27, 1861.

Fisher, Augustus, Private, August 27, 1861.

Fisher, John, Private, August 27, 1861.

Foster, John L., Private, September 6, 1861.

Froelich, Valentine, Private, August 27, 1861.

Gephart, George W., Private, August 27, 1861.*

Goulden, William, Private, August 27, 1861.*

Gross, Anthony, Private, August 27, 1861.

Hartsock, Henry H., Private, August, 27, 1861.

Heintza, William, Private, August 27, 1861.

Hite, Jacob, Private, August 27, 1861.

Hiteshaw, James M., Private, August 27, 1861.

Holton, John, Private, August 27, 1861.*

Hooper, Lewis, Private, August 27,1861.

Howard, James A., Private, August 27, 1861.

Hughes, Joseph, Private, September, 1861.

Ilein. Francis, Private, August 27, 1861.*

Irons, George S., Private, August 27, 1861.

Irvine, William., Private, August 27, 1861.

Jackson, Jonathan L., Private, August 27, 1861.*

Jackson, William H., Private, August 27, 1861.*

Johnson, James, Private, September 17, 1861.*

Johnston, Wilson, Private, August 27, 1861.*

Judy, Richard, Private, August 27, 1861.*

Keller, John W., Private, October 7, 1861.*

Kirtley, Joseph, Private, August 27, 1861.

Lauder, Samuel B., Private, August 27, 1861.

McDonald, Phillip T., Private, September 3, 1861.

McKee, James A., Corporal, August 27, 1861.

Middleton, William, Private, August 27, 1861.*

Mills, Patrick, Private, August 27, 1861.

Mintdrop, Henry, Private, August 27, 1861.

Monnett, Norman N., Private, August 27, 1861.

Mulligan, Luke, Private, August 27, 1861.

Murray, William H., Private, August 27, 1861.

Musgrove, Daniel C., Private, August 27, 1861.

Myers, Thomas F., Private, August 27, 1861.

Noonan, Thomas L., Private, November 5, 1861.

Nunimaker, Theodore, Private, August 27, 1861.

Oliver, John, Private, September 4, 1861.

O'Neal, Hugh, Private, August 27, 1861.

Potts, John W., Private, August 27, 1861.*

Pressman, Peter, Private, August 27, 1861.

Rhind, John W., Private, August 27, 1861.*

Rose, William M., Private, September 5, 1861.

Rowe, James W., Private, August 27, 1861.

Shaw, Oliver, Private, August 27, 1861.

Sheriff, David, Private, September 20, 861.

Shipley, Samuel, Private, August 27, 1861.*

Shoebridge, Benjamin C., Private, September 4, 1861.

Shuck, Henry C., Private, August 27, 1861.*

Shupe, John, Private, August 27, 1861.*

Sills, George W., Private, September 5, 1861.

Sills, John A., Private, August 27, 1861.

Sloop, Isaiah, Private, August 27, 1861.

Smouse, Josephus, Private, August 27, 1861.

Sommerkamp, Charles F., Private, September 26, 1861.

Stevenson, George H., Private, August 27, 1861.

Sullivan, James M., Private, September 19, 1861.

Syers, Emanuel, Private, September 14, 1861.

Teeters, William W., Private, August 27, 1861.*

Troxell, Thomas, Private, August 27, 1861.

Turner, John, Private, August 27, 1861.*

Twigg, John F. Private, August 27, 1861.*

Ward, George W., Private, August 27, 1861.

Warner, Louis, Private, September 4, 1861.

Weber, John, Private, August 27, 1861.

Wigfield, Isaac, Private, August 27, 1861.*

Wilhide, Oliver R., Private, August 27, 1861.*

Zaph, John, Private, September 16, 1861.

*Transferred to Company A.

COMPANY F

Alens, William, Private, August 26, 1861.

Anthony, Conrad, Private, August 31, 1861.

Barker, George, Private, August 31, 1861.

Beard, Lewis, Private, September 17, 1861.

Bectol, Henry C., Private, August 31, 1861.

Bowers, John T., Private, September 4, 1861.*

Brady, Joshua J., Private, August 31, 1861.*

Burlin, Jefferson, Private, August 31, 1861.

Buzzard, George D., Private, August 31, 1861.*

Capp, George E., Private, December 20, 1861.

Capp, John P., Private, August 31, 1861.

Colbert, Jonathan W., Private, August 31, 1861.

Compton, Ezekiel, Private, August 31, 1861.

Compton, William, Private, August 31, 1861.

Corbitt, Francis T., Private, September 17, 1861.

Creek, Charles W., Private, September 4, 1861.*

Cross, James Francis, Private, August 31, 1861.*

Dawson Frederick W., Private, November 17, 1861.

Dawson, Moses, Private, December 18, 1861.

Dawson, Thomas H. B., Private, October 13, 1861.

Duckwall, John W., Private, September 11, 1861.

Duckwall, William, Private, August 31, 1861.

Farris, John, Private, September 11, 1861.

Folson, Jacob, Private, August 31, 1861.

Folson, John W., Private, August 31, 1861.

Foster, George, Private, August 31, 1861.

Friskey, Lewis, Private, September 4, 1861.

Gallaher, Joshua S., Private, August 31, 1861.*

Gallion, William R., Private, August 31, 1861.*

Ganoe, John W., Private, August 31, 1861.

Givault, Edward R., Private, September 9, 1861.

Graves, Charles, Private, September 5, 1861.*

Halbert, John D., Private, December 18, 1861.

Halbert, William H., Private, August 31, 1861.

Henry, John W., Private, August 31, 1861.

Henry, Levi, Private, August 31, 1861.

Hoffman, Simon, Private, August 31, 1861.

Higgs, Henry Z., Private, August 29, 1861.

Jackson, James E., Private, August 31, 1861.*

James, Elisha, Private, August 31, 1861.

Lutman, David H., Private, September 6, 1861.

Lutman, George W., Private, September 6, 1861.

Lutman, Henry, Private, December 18, 1861.

McBee, Franklin, Private, September 6, 1861.

McBee, Harrison P., Private, September 25, 1861.*

McBee, Henry C., Private, September 6, 1861.

McBee, Joseph H., Private, September 6, 1861.

McBee, William T., Private, September 4, 1861.

McCoy, Jacob W. W., Private, September 2, 1861.

Michael, Joseph L., Private, August 31, 1861.

Michael, Henry H., Private, September 6, 1861.

Moreland, Basil, Private, August 31, 1861.

Norris, Josephus, Private, December 18, 1861.

Ortman, Benjamin B., Private, August 31, 1861.

Picken, William, Private, August 31, 1861.

Pickens, Christopher, Private, September 23, 1861.

Poisal, Adam P. S., Private, August 31, 1861.

Post, Abraham, Private, August 31, 1861.

Price, Van A., Private, August 31, 1861.

Prichard, Parker, Private, August 31, 1861.

Richards, Isaac, Private, September 13, 1861.

Roach, Joseph, Private, August 31, 1861.

Sagle, William H., Private, August 31, 1861.

Shank, Samuel, Private, August 31, 1861.

Sheppard, William, Private, August 31, 1861.

Shockley, George P., Private, September 13, 1861.

Simpson, John W., Private, August 31, 1861.

Smith, Charles D., Private, August 31, 1861.

Sowders, Michael, Private, September 16, 1861.*

Sowders, Peter, Private, September 13, 1861.

Spaulding, Francis I., Private, August 31, 1861.

Spottlemyre, Joseph B., Private, September 25, 1861.

Switzer, George R., Private, September 4, 1861.

Switzer, John H., Private, September 18, 1861.

Tabler, John A., Private, August 31, 1861.

Thomas, Erasmus T., Private, August 31, 1861.

Tower, Edward H., Sergeant, September 4, 1861.

Tritapoa, William, Private, August 31, 1861.

Waugh, George L., Private, August 31, 1861.

Waugh, James S., Private, August 31, 1861.

Waugh, John W., Private, October 1, 1861.*

Waugh, Thomas W., Private, August 31, 1861.

Webster, David, Private, October 5, 1861.

Wells, Joseph D., Private, September 13, 1861.

Wharton, Fielding, Private, November 17, 1861.*

Wharton, Samuel, Private, August 31, 1861.

Whitacre, Edward, Private, September 23, 1861.
Whitacre, Meredith, Private, September 23, 1861.
Widmyer, Samuel S., Private, August 31, 1861.
Yider, Joseph, Private, September 13, 1861.
Yost, John W., Private, Private, September 4, 1861.
Yost, Levi, Private, August 31, 1861.
Youngblood, John W., Private, August 31, 1861.
Zeilor, Cornelius, Private, September 13, 1861.
Zeilor, George, Private, September 13, 1861.
Zeilor, Pendleton, Private, September 13, 1861.

*Transferred to Company C.

COMPANY G

Barnes, Samuel, Private, August 31, 1861.

Bauman, Joel, Private, August 31, 1861

Berg, Augustus, Private, September 16, 1861.

Berwinkle, George, Private, August 28, 1861.

Berwinkle, Henry, Private, August 31, 1861.

Berwinkle, William, Private, August 28, 1861.*

Boyer, Josiah, Private, August 31, 1861.

Boyer, Levi L., Private, August 31, 1861.

Boyer, Peter, Private, August 31, 1861.

Boyer, Samuel J., Private, August 31, 1861.

Brant, Samuel J., Private, August 31, 1861.

Breakiron, Joshua, Private, August 31, 1861.

Browns, Jacob, Private, August 31, 1861.

Caton, Robert, Private, August 31, 1861.

Cowgill, James A., Private, August 31, 1861.

Crosby, Nathaniel, Private, August 31, 1861.

Dannels, John, Private, August 31, 1861.

Davis, Richard, Private, August 31, 1861.

Devore, John, Private, August 31, 1861.

Dick, Robert, Private, August 31, 1861.

Dolan, Lawrence, Private, August 31, 1861.

Dougherty, Daniel, Private, August 31, 1861.

Dummel, Ignatius, Private, September 9, 1861.

Durst, Henry, Private, August 31, 1861.

Evans, John J., Private, August 31, 1861.

Foster, Lemuel, Private, August 31, 1861.

Frechloch, Adam, Private, September 16, 1861.

Frechloch, Sebastian, Private, September 16, 1861.

Garey, Lloyd, Private, August 31, 1861.

Goodwin, Peter, Private, August 31, 1861.

Graham, Thomas, Private, August 31, 1861.**

Gramlich, Jonathan M., Private, August 31, 1861.

Haley, John, Private, August 31, 1861.

Hile, Franklin, Private, August 31, 1861.

Hoble, Casper, Private, August 31, 1861.

Horner, Henry, Private, August 31, 1861.*

Horner, John, Private, September 20, 1861*.

Hutson, George W., Private, August 31, 1861.

Johnston, William H., Private, August 31, 1861.

Kaub, Joseph J., Private, September 18, 1861.

Keller, Jeremiah, Private, August 31, 1861.

Keller, Justus, Private, August 31, 1861.

King, Joseph, Private, September 16, 1861.

Larkin, Mathias J., Private, August 31, 1861.

Leidig, George, Private, August 31, 1861.

Lewis, William D., Private, August 31, 1861.

Lochead, James, Private, August 31, 1861.

Lyburger, William, Private, August 31, 1861.

Maher, Thomas, Private, August 31, 1861.

Malone, John, Private, August 31, 1861.

May, George, Private, August 16, 1861.

McCullough, Robert, Private, August 31, 1861.*

McEllfish, Brooks, Private, August 31, 1861.

McGirr, Matthew, Private, August 31, 1861.

McKenzie, Dennis, Private, August 31, 1861.

McQuillen, Hiram, Private, August 31, 1861.

Mertins, Charles, Private, September 16, 1861.

Morrison, William, Private, August 31, 1861.

Murrie, David, Private, September 20, 1861.

Murrie, William, Private, September 20. 1861.

Nelson, John, Private, August 31, 1861.

Opitz, Earnest, Private, September 16, 1861.

Orr, Andrew, Private, September 1, 1861.

Orr, James, Private, Private, August 31, 1861.

Owen, Benjamin, Private, August 31, 1861.

Owens, George, Private, August 31, 1861.

Platter, George W., Private, August 31, 1861.

Rimes, John, Private, August 31, 1861.

Rohman, George, Private, August 31, 1861.*

Shaw, Freedom, Private, August 31, 1861.

Shumesser, Henry, Private, October, 16, 1861.

Shoemaker, Harman, Private, August 31, 1861.

Simpson, David, Private, August 31, 1861.

Simpson, Elisha, Private, August 31, 1861.

Simpson, James, Private, August 31, 1861.

Staub, John F., Private, August 31, 1861.

Stocks, Samuel, Private, August 31, 1861.

Timmons, Joseph, Private, August 1, 1861.

Twigg, Michael C. S., Private, August 31, 1861.

Webb, Joseph, Private, August 31, 1861.

Weisbaugh, John, Private, August 31, 1861.

Welsh, James, Private, August 31, 1861.

Welsh, Joseph, Private, August 31, 1861.

Weinold, Conrad, Private, August 31, 1861.*

Zimmerly, Samuel, Private, August 31, 1861.

*Transferred to Company A.

**Transferred to Company C.

COMPANY H

Albright, Conrad, September 4, 1861.

Allison, Robert H., Private, August 31, 1861.

Bateman, Nathaniel C., Private, August 31, 1861.

Beltz, William W. W., Private, September 10, 1861.

Brant, Dennis B., Private, August 31, 1861.

Brant, Oliver P., Private, September 28, 1861.

Bray, Caleb, Private, August 31, 1861.

Brown, John W., Private, August 31, 1861.

Buntz, Charles S. W., Private, August 31, 1861.*

Carleton, Henry M., Private, August 31, 1861.

Coffee, Thomas, Private, September 12, 1861.

Connell, Zachariah, Private, September 4, 1861,

Cook, Levi, Private, September 10, 1861.

Cook, Samuel A., Private, September 21, 1861.

Couter, Jacob R., Private, September 16, 1861.**

Cubbage, Charles H., Private, September 4, 1861.

Davis, George W., Private, August 31, 1861.

Davis, Samuel F., Private, August 31, 1861.

Davis, Thomas, Private, August 31, 1861.

Deeter, Samuel, Private, August 31, 1861.

Ellenberger, Michael E., Private, August 31, 1861.*

Evans, Benjamin, Private, September 28, 1861.

Farner, Harman, Private, September 30, 1861.

Feaga, Charles H., Private, August 31, 1861.

Feaga, David F., Private, August 31, 1861.

Fink, Lewis, Private, September 4, 1861.

Fisher, Charles, Private, September 12, 1861.

Fisher, Conrad, Private, October 2, 1861.

Frantz, Frederick J., Private, September 18, 1861.

Furstenberg, Joseph M., Private, August 31, 1861.

Frethey, Gideon G., Private, September 12, 1861.

Graves, Dennis, Private, August 31, 1861.

Gonden, Lewis N., Private, August 31, 1861.*

Gouden, Peter, Private, August 31, 1861.*

Handle, Jacob, Private, August 31, 1861.

Haslacker, Anthony, Private, August 31, 1861.*

Hennicker, Christopher, Private, August 31, 1861.

Hensell, Walter S., Private, August 31, 1861.

Herpick, John C. G., Private, September 24, 1861.

Hilkey, James S., Private, September 4, 1861.

Hill, James T., Private, August 31, 1861.

Hite, George F., Private, September 3, 1861.

Holmes, Lewis, Private, August 31, 1861.

Hopwood, Joshua, Private, September 25, 1861.

Houck, Joseph, Private, September 7, 1861.

Hoyle, Jacob, Private, August 31, 1861.

Humbertson, George, Private, August 31, 1861.

Isaacs, Henry C., Private, August 31, 1861.

Johnson, Thomas, Private, August 31, 1861.

Johnson, Thomas, Private, August 31, 1861.

Kegg, Levi R., Private, October 29, 1861.

Keplinger, Jacob M., Private, September 4, 1861.

Knee, Phillip, Private, September 7, 1861.*

Knorr, George T. R., Private, August 31, 1861.*

Knorr, Joseph P., Private, August 31, 1861.*

Kopp, John, Private, September 19, 1861.

Leonard, Phillip, Private, August 31, 1861.

Magee, Daniel, Private, August 31, 1861.

Markel, Samuel, Private, September 18, 1861.

Martz, George H., Private, September 18, 1861.

May, Daniel H., Private, September 10, 1861.

May, Samuel, Private, August 31, 1861.

Motter, John W., Private, August 31, 1861.

Murvine, John, Private, August 31, 1861.

Myers, James, Private, September 19, 1861.*

Nine, Francis M., Private, September 4, 1861.

Ohr, William D., Private, August 31, 1861.*

Palmer, Justus F., Private, August 31, 1861.

Pelton, John, Private, August 31, 1861.

Penn, William J., Private, August 31, 1861.

Pepple, Daniel, Private, August 31, 1861.

Poole, Arthur A., Private, August 31, 1861.

Pyfer, Simon, Private, September 18, 1861.

Ringler, George W., Private, September 20, 1861.

Ringler, Henry, Private, October 15, 1861.

Ringler, Joshua, Private, August 31, 1861.

Rizer, John W. W., Private, August 31, 1861.

Rohm, James H., Private, August 31, 1861.

Sears, John T., Private, September 18, 1861.

Sears, Josiah W., Private, September 18, 1861.

Shank, Edward A., Private, September 7, 1861.

Shriver, Henry, Private, August 31, 1861.

Shroyer, Daniel J., Private, August 31, 1861.

Shuck, John H., Private, August 31, 1861.

Shuck William S., Private, August 31, 1861.

Smith, James L., Private, September 25, 1861.

Snyder, John W., Private, September 11, 1861.

Spaughey, William, Private, August 31, 1861.

Steiner, John W., Private, August 31, 1861.

Stoner, Samuel, Private, October 15, 1861.

Stover, Shryer, Private, September 12, 1861.

Taylor, William J., Private, August 31, 1861.

Turner, Benjamin, Private, September 18, 1861.

Turner, John W., Private, September 4, 1861.

Valentine, Benjamin R., Private, September 7, 1861.

Veatch, William, Private, September 4, 1861.*

Walker, John L., Private, August 31, 1861.

Wallace, John, Private, August 31, 1861.

Weis, George W., Private, august 31, 1861.

Wilson, James, Private, September 4, 1861.

Wolf, Samuel G., Private, September 4, 1861.

*Transferred to Company A.

**Transferred to Company E.

COMPANY I

Amtire, George, Private, September 9, 1861.

Arnold, Dennis, Private, October 31, 1861.

Balson, James S. E., Private, September 9, 1861.

Bateson, Jonathan W., Private, October 31, 1861.

Bittinger, Noah, Private, October 31, 1861.

Brown, Thomas, Private, October 31, 1861.

Browning, Richard T., Private, October 31, 1861.*

Burk, Mahlon, Private, October 31, 1861.*

Casey, Samuel, Private, October, 31, 1861.

Casteel, Francis T., Private, October 31, 1861.

Cessna, Joseph, Private, October 31, 1861.

Cross, Charles H., Private, October 31, 1861.

Cross, Thomas, Private, September 11, 1861.

Dawson, Norman B., Private, October 31, 1861.

Dunham, William, Private, October 31, 1861.

Filler, John H., Private, October 31, 1861.*

Finnegan, Michael, Private, October 31, 1861.*

Forsythe, John M., Private, October 31, 1861.

Frantz, Alfred L., Private, October 31, 1861.*

Frantz, Joseph H., Private, October 31, 1861.

Frantz, Thomas P., Private, October 31, 1861.

Frantz, William B., Private, October 31, 1861.

Frazee, Jonathan T., Private, October 31, 1861.

Friend, Andrew C., Private, October 31, 1861.*

Friend, Andrew G., Private, October 31, 1861.*

Friend, Elijah M., Private, October 31, 1861.

Friend, Francis M., Private, October 31, 1861.*

Friend, Hanson B., Corporal, October 31, 1861.

Friend, Reese E., Private, October 31, 1861.*

Friend, William E., Private, October 31, 1861.

Friend, William H. H., Private, October 31, 1861.*

Garletz, George W., Private, October 31, 1861.*

Garletz, John, Private, October 31, 1861.*

Gephart, Harrison, Private, October 31, 1861.*

Glotfelty, Thadeus, Private, October 31, 1861.

Green, John, Private, October 31, 1861.

Griffith, Joab, Private, October 31, 1861.

Hartman, Daniel, Private, October 31, 1861.

Hawthorn, Levi, Private, October 31, 1861.

Hay, John, Private, October 31, 1861.*

Hershberger, Abraham J., Private, November 10, 1861.*

Hershberger, Elijah, Private, October 31, 1861.*

Hite, Joseph E., Private, October 31, 1861.

Hoop, Henry, Private, October 31, 1861.

Hough, Howard, Private, October 31, 1861.

Hough, Jonathan T., Private, October 31, 1861.

Houston, Charles A., Private, October 31, 1861.

Jenkins, Alfred, Private, October 31, 1861.*

Kelly, Alexander, Private, October 31, 1861.

Knapp, Christopher J., Private, October 31, 1861.*

Lowdermilk, Samuel P., Private, October 31, 1861.*

Lyons, William, Private, October 31, 1861.

Martinch, Louis, Private, September 13, 1861.

McKenzie, Jacob P., Private, October 31, 1861.*

McKinzie, John, Private, October 31, 1861.*

McMullen, Jeremiah, Private, October 31, 1861.

Merrill, Noah, Private, October 31, 1861.*

Morris, Thomas, Private, October 31, 1861.

Preston, Dennis, Private, October 31, 1861.

Preston, Meshack, Private, October 31, 1861.

Preston, William, Private, October 31, 1861.

Quick, James, Private, October 31, 1861.

Raferty, Patrick, Private, October 31, 1861.*

Rice, Samuel, Private, October 31, 1861.

Shroyer, William, Private, October 31, 1861.*

Shunk, Benjamin, Private, October 31, 1861.

Sloan, David, Private, October 31, 1861.

Smith, Charles, Private, October 31, 1861.

Snowden, Adam D., Private, October 31, 1861.

Thayer, Charles H., Sergeant, October 31, 1861.

Turner, Harvey, Private, October 31, 1861.*

Uphold, Calvin, Private, October 31, 1861.*

Uphold, James, Private, October 31, 1861.*

Uphold, James L., Private, October 31, 1861.*

Wable, Noah, Private, October 31, 1861.

Washington, George, Private, October 31, 1861.

Wentling, George, Private, October 31, 1861.*

White, William P., Private, October 31, 1861.

White, Wilson, Private, October 31, 1861.**

Williams, John, Private, October 31, 1861.*

Wilson, Andrew J., Private, October 31, 1861.

Wilson, Joseph D., Private, October 31, 1861.*

*Transferred to Company B.

** Transferred to Company C.

COMPANY K

Allison, John, Private, October 31, 1861.

Arnold, Samuel H., Private, October 31, 1861.*

Baker, Christian, Private, October 31, 1861.

Baker, David, Private, September 18, 1861.

Beal, Jeremiah, Private, October 31, 1861.

Beal, John D., Private, September 18, 1861.

Bickford, Albert, Private, September 18, 1861.

Bittner, Silas J., Private, October 31, 1861.

Boyer, Benjamin, Private, October 31, 1861.

Buckey, Jacob H., Private, October 31, 1861.*

Burtenett, James W., Private, October 7, 1861.

Caton, George, Private, October 31, 1861.

Cook, Jesse, Private, October 31, 1861.*

Crosby, John, Private, September 18, 1861.

Croston, Thomas H., Private, November 21, 1861.*

Dehaven, Dennis, Private, October 31, 1861.

Dehaven, William S., Private, October 31, 1861.

Denton, John O., Private, October 31, 1861.

Dorsey, Augustus, Private, October 31, 1861.

Facenbaker, William, Private, September 18, 1861.*

Finley, David, Private, September 18, 1861.*

Folk, Thomas J., Private, October 31, 1861.

Folk, Thomas J., Private, October 31, 1861.

Folk, William, Private, October 31, 1861.

Gourmer, William H., Private, October 31, 1861.

Havim, Martin, Private, October 31, 1861.

Hicks, William a., Private, October 31, 1861.

Johnson, James, Private, October 31, 1861.*

Johnston, James, Private, September 18, 1861.*

Kendle, John, Private, September 23, 1861.

Kesler, Peter, Private, October 31, 1861.

Kinsey, John B., Private, October 31, 1861.*

Krigleine, George P., Private, October 31, 1861.

Logsden, Joseph, Private, September 18, 1861.

Logsden, Raphael, Private, September 18, 1861.

Martens, Joachim C., Private, October 31, 1861.

McKnight, Simeon, Private, October 31, 1861.

Moser, John, Private, September 18, 1861.

Moser, Reuben, Private, September 18, 1861.

Petrie, Samuel M., Private, September 18, 1861.

Schmidt, Conrad, Private, October 31, 1861.

Schritchfeld, Samuel, Private, October 31, 1861.

Shockey, Christian, Private, September 18, 1861.*

Shoemaker, Daniel, Private, October 31, 1861.

Stacer, John, Private, October 31, 1861.*

Stanley, Isaac W., Private, November 26, 1861.*

Stanley, John R., Private, November 26, 1861.*

Sturtz, George, Private, October 31, 1861.

Taylor, William H., Private, December 10, 1861.*

Taylor, Wilson L., Private, October 31, 1861.

Tennant, Thomas, Private, October 31, 1861.

Tharp, Jacob, Private, October 31, 1861.

Troutman, Daniel, Private, September 18, 1861.*

Valentine, John, Private, October 31, 1861.

Walker, Alexander, Private, October 31, 1861.*

Winebrenner, George W., Private, October 31, 1861.*

Winter, John N., Private, October 31, 1861.

Witt, George, Private, October 31, 1861.

Yates, Thomas, Private, October 31, 1861.*

*Transferred to Company C.

THIRD REGIMENT
POTOMAC HOME BRIGADE

COMPANY A

Alexander, William, Private, September 12, 1861.

Andrew, Joseph, Private, September 12, 1861.

Arnold, Dominick, Corporal, September 27, 1861.

Ayers, Henry, Private, September 12, 1861.

Bearers, Norman, Teamster, December 12, 1861.

Broadwaters, Noble W., Private, September 23, 1861.

Cage, Andrew, Private, September 27, 1861.

Coleman, Lewis J., Corporal, December 31, 1861.

Conrad, Heine, Private, December 31, 1861.

Commer, Edward, , Private, September 23, 1861.

Creihner, Charles, Private, December 31, 1861.

Crentzburg, Valentine, Private, October 15, 1861.

Cress, George, Private, September 24, 1861.

Crowley, Patrick, Private, September 27, 1861.

Dailey, Patrick, Private, October 3, 1861.

Davis, Benjamin, Private, December 31, 1861.

Deusy, Thomas, Private, September 16, 1861.

Dick, Roberts, Private, December 31, 1861.

Dimpsey, Thomas, Private, October 31, 1861.

Facenbaker, Jonathan, Private, November 6, 1861.

Fagan, Bartholomew, Private, December 31, 1861.

Fazenbaker, Andrew J., Private, November 6, 1861.

Gannon, Michael, Private, September 23, 1861.

George, William E., Corporal, September 12, 1861.

Gilbert, Thomas, Private, September 12, 1861.

Green, Benjamin F., Private, September 23, 1861.

Harding, Josiah, Private, November 10, 1861.

Hearnon, Michael, Private, September 23, 1861.

Henry, James, Private, September 23, 1861.

Innskeep, Henry M., Private, September 12, 1861.

Jacobs, Matthew, Private, September 12, 1861.

Jones, Alexander, Private, September 25, 1861.

Kight, Silas, Private, September 12, 1861.

Kight, Zadock, Private, September 23, 1861.

Kimmell, Joseph, Corporal, October 31, 1861.

Lagsdon, David J., Private, September 23, 1861.

Lagsdon, William, Private, September 16, 1861.

Lamon, Daniel B., Private, December 9, 1861.

Laton, Peter, Private, December 31, 1861.

Layton, William, Private, September 16, 1861.

Maloy, Anthony, Private, September 16, 1861.

Martin, Joseph, Private, December 31, 1861.

McCarroll, Patrick, Corporal, September 23, 1861.

McCrobie, Francis M., Private, November 26, 1861.

McCrobie, Hampton, Private, November 26, 1861.

Metts, Benjamin T., Private, October 26, 1861.

Metts, Isaac, Private, October 24, 1861.

Metts, John H., Private, December 31, 1861.

Metts, Joseph, Private, September 23, 1861.

Miller, Galloway, Private, September 12, 1861.

O'Brian, Patrick, Private, September 12, 1861.

O'Brian, John, Private, September 16, 1861.

O'Malley, Patrick P., Sergeant, December 27, 1861.

Orr, Robert, Private, September 16, 1861.

Parker, John T., Musician, December 18, 1861.

Pashaw, Julius, Private, December 31, 1861.

Patterson, John, Private, December 1, 1861.

Penman, William, Private, September 23, 1861.

Powers, James, Private, December 10, 1861.

Rhodes, Jonathan W., Private, December 31, 1861.

Rhodes, William H., Private, September 27, 1861.

Samson, Hugh, Private, December 31, 1861.

Scott, William, Private, December 31, 1861.

Sharon, James, 1st Sergeant, December 13, 1861.

Shaw, James P., Private, September 12, 1861.

Shearer, David D., Sergeant, September 23, 1861.

Shearer, James, 1st Sergeant, September 23, 1861.

Shoe, John, Private, September 12, 1861.

Stewart, James, Private, October 9, 1861.

Uphold, William, Corporal, October 25, 1861.

Ward, Martin, Private, September 23, 1861.

Warner, William, Private, October 25, 1861.

Warnick, William, Private, October 25, 1861.

Weimer, Joseph, Corporal, December 9, 1861.

Wilburn, Ralph, Private, December 31, 1861.

Wilburn, Tilghman H., Private, September 23, 1861.

Williams, George, Corporal, September 12, 1861.

Willison, James H., Private, September 24, 1861.

COMPANY B

Allison, William H., Private, December 11, 1861.

Andros, Adam, Private, October 23, 1861.

Baels, Adam S., Private, October 18, 1861.

Barber, George W., Private, October 11, 1861.

Barber, John H., Private, October 30, 1861.

Barney, Isaac, Private, September 28, 1861.

Barney, John H., 1st Sergeant, November 9, 1861.

Betty, Henry, Jr., Private, October 23, 1861.

Bingaman, Levi F., Corporal, November 9, 1861.

Booth, William, Private, October 28, 1861.

Bowers, George W., Private, December 3, 1861.

Bowser, Charles W., Private, November 19, 1861.

Breakall, John, Private, October 10, 1861.

Brenaman, Martin, Private, December 1, 1861.

Brooks, William H., Private, November 1, 1861.

Bush, George W., Corporal, October 23, 1861.

Bush, George W., Private, December 23, 1861.

Byer, Samuel C., Corporal, October 11, 1861.

Byer, William J., Private, October 22, 1861.

Carson, John T., Sergeant, October 11, 1861.

Cassel, John H., Private, November 11, 1861.

Chippy, William, Corporal, October 19, 1861.

Cook, James A., Sergeant, October 26, 1861.

Cooper, James A., Private, December 12, 1861.

Covalt, Bethnel, Private, September 28, 1861.

Coy, Henry, Private, December 20, 1861.

Curley, David, Private, November 4, 1861.

Curtis, Isadore, Private, October 15, 1861.

Daywalt, Martin, Private, October 12, 1861.

Devilbiss, Frederick, Private, October 18, 1861.

Devilbiss, Jonathan H., Private, November 9, 1861.

Devilbiss, Joseph, Private, November 23, 1861.

Dimon, George, Private, December 9, 1861.

Doyle, David, Corporal, November 12, 1861.

Eichelberger, William H., Private, December 30, 1861.

Flougher, Jonathan C., Private, November 12, 1861.

Fohner, Enoch H., Private, September 28, 1861.

Foreback, Felix, Sergeant, September 28, 1861.

Gerlach, George W., Corporal, November 23, 1861.

Goodrich, Matthew, Private, November 21, 1861.

Greenwalt, Martin, Private, December 3, 1861.

Gresser, William, Corporal, November 12, 1861.

Hagerman, Andrew, Private, October 14, 1861.

Hale, George W., Private, October 30, 1861.

Hall, James W., Private, December 11, 1861.

Halmon, Henry, Private, October 14, 1861.

Harning, Peter, Private, October 19, 1861.

Hedding, Ephraim G., Private, September 28, 1861.

Hedding, Noah, Private, October 12, 1861.

Hipner, Daniel, Private, September 28, 1861.

Hipner, Frederick, Private, November 4, 1861.

Hockensmith, John, Private, November 9, 1861.

Hoffer, Michael, Corporal, October 30, 1861.

Hoffer, John, Private, November 5, 1861.

Hughes, James E., Corporal, December 15, 1861.

Hull, Jacob, Sergeant, November 25, 1861.

Krunkelton, John W., Private, December 21, 1861.

Kuhn, Daniel, Private, October 26, 1861.

Leighty, Jacob C., Private, October 21, 1861.

Linn, Hugh, Teamster, September 28, 1861.

Linn, Reilly, Private, September 28, 1861.

Linn, William, Private, September 28, 1861.

Lizer, Henry, Private, December 21, 1861.

Lowrey, John, Private, September 28, 1861.

Lowrey, Joseph, Private, September 28, 1861.

Mann, Joshua, Private, October 23, 1861.

Marker, Benjamin, Private, November 6, 1861.

Marker, Samuel, Private, October 25, 1861.

Marsh, John H., Private, December 10, 1861.

McAway, Jonathan B., Private, October 30, 1861.

McClellan, John D. C., Private, December 21, 1861.

McCoy, David W., Private, December 30, 1861.

McCulloch, Jeremiah, Private, October 26, 1861.

McKinsey, William, Private, November 12, 1861.

Meisner, James, Private, December 30, 1861.

Meisner, Solomon W., Private, October 23, 1861.

Mellott, Frederick, Private, November 25, 1861.

Mellott, Peter, Private, November 9, 1861.

Meyers, Lewis, Private, November 8, 1861.

Meyers, William, Private, November 6, 1861.

Miller, John, Private, November 6, 1861

Miller, John, Private, November 4, 1861.

Miller, Michael, Private, November 6, 1861.

Moxley, William, Private, October 30, 1861.

Myers, Reuben, Private, October 23, 1861.

Oaker, Charles, Corporal, October 14, 1861.

Peters, Lewis, Private, November 19, 1861.

Pittman, Sylvester, Private, November 16, 1861.

Powell, Abraham, Private, October 16, 1861.

Powell, Bazil M., Private, December 21, 1861.

Reckner, Josephus, Private, December 28, 1861.

Ross, Daniel, Private, December 27, 1861.

Ross, James, Private, November 19, 1861.

Saylor, Daniel W., Private, October 27, 1861.

Scott, Daniel W., Private, November 7, 1861.

Seigler, Abraham, Private, December 3, 1861.

Seigler, William, Private, December 30, 1861.

Shafer, Abdon B., Musician, October 19, 1861.

Shafer, John G., Private, September 28, 1861.

Shetrompf, Jonathan, Private, October 28, 1861.

Shipway, George E., Private, September 28, 1861.

Shipway, Jonathan C., Private, November 16, 1861.

Simmons, John A., Sergeant, October 24, 1861.

Simmons, Thomas, Sergeant, November 11, 1861.

Sipes, George W., Corporal, November 20, 1861.

Slayman, Samuel, Private, October 27, 1861.

Smith, Nathan P. R., Private, October 21, 1861.

Spinger, George W., Private, November 8, 1861.

Sponsler, George W., Private, November 5, 1861.

Sponsler, Solomon, Private, November 5, 1861.

Startzman, George W., Sergeant, October 18, 1861.

Stipp, Abraham V., Private, October 15, 1861.

Thomas, Jonathan F., Private, November 18, 1861.

Tschuday, David, Private, October 15, 1861.

Wassen, Jacob, 1st Sergeant, October 23, 1861.

Weaver, George, Private, November 4, 1861.

Welling, James, Private, November 7, 1861.

Wilman, Julius T. C., Private, December 6, 1861.

Whitford, Jonathan H., Private, November 11, 1861.

Wolf, Samuel, Private, November 26, 1861.

Young, Abraham E., Private, November 12, 1861.

COMPANY C

Arnold, John A., Private, December 23, 1861.

Biderman, James H. D., Private, November 16, 1861.

Brown, James, Private, December 10, 1861.

Cook, James H., Corporal, October 26, 1861.

Cook, John W., Sergeant, October 19, 1861.

Engle, David, Private, December 24, 1861.

Enix, Randolph, Private, October 5, 1861.

Fasenbaker, George W., Private, September 12, 1861.

Hagg, Valentine, Private, December 28, 1861.

Hendershott, Samuel G., Sergeant, October 12, 1861.

Kirk, George, Private, September 19, 1861.

Lyshon, William, Private, December 18, 1861.

Metts, Isaac N. W., Corporal, September 14, 1861.

McDonnell, Michael, Corporal, October 8, 1861.

McQuade, James, Sergeant, October 2, 1861.

Mullen, Hugh, Private, December 23, 1861.

Murphy, Josiah F., Corporal, October 23, 1861.

Myers, William, Private, November 6, 1861.

Owens, Joseph, Private, November 2, 1861.

Pittman, Joseph K., Sergeant, November 19, 1861.

Pullman, James, Private, December 10, 1861.

Rye, Edward C. M., Private, October 11, 1861.

Sager, Abraham, Private, November 6, 1861.

Sliger, Lucian, Private, December 10, 1861.

Tasker, James W., Private, November 14, 1861.

Teets, Ezra, Private, October 25, 1861.

Wilson, Robert C., Private, December 16, 1861.

Wolford, Josiah, Private, December 31, 1861.

Woodward, Presley, October 23, 1861.

COMPANY D

Abernathy, Ephraim, Private, September 17, 1861.

Alexander, Elias, Private, October 23, 1861.

Barkholder, Samson, Private, September 14, 1861.

Beam, John J., Private, October 29, 1861.

Bedour, Henry F., Private, October 7, 1861.

Black, John, Private, December 10, 1861.

Brown, James, Private, December 20, 1861.

Brady, Michael T., Private, December 19, 1861.

Bray, John, Private, December 17, 1861.

Bruce, James D., Private, October 16, 1861.

Buckbee, Benjamin F., Private, October 29, 1861.

Coleman, Simeon D., 1st Sergeant, September 19, 1861.

Comp, Levi, Private, November 4, 1861.

Cubbage, Benjamin S., Private, August 28, 1861.

Cummins, George, Private, September 24, 1861.

Darrah, Augustus, Private, September 26, 1861.

Durst, Casper, Private, November 11, 1861.

Durst, Jeremiah, Sergeant, November 11, 1861.

Engle, David, Private, December 24, 1861.

Engle, Perry, Private, September 12, 1861.

Faulkenstine, John J., Private, December 30, 1861.

Finnegan, Amos E., Musician, September 12, 1861.

Ford, John T., Private, September 12, 1861.

Friend, Joseph H., Private, November 24, 1861.

Friend, Benjamin F., Private, November 24, 1861.

Gilpin, John, Corporal, September 26, 1861.

Hager, John, Private, October 9, 1861.

Haring, Peter, Sergeant, October 19, 1861.

Harvey, Samson, Private, October 19, 1861.

Harvey, William L., Private, October 3, 1861.

Hoffman, Henry, Private, October 23, 1861.

Hogan, Patrick O., Private, September 12, 1861.

Holstead, James F., Private, October 31, 1861.

Holstead, Samuel, Private, October 15, 1861.

Holstead, William B., Private, November 8, 1861.

House, Amon, Corporal, October 15, 1861.

Howell, Jefferson, Private, September 14, 1861.

Janney, William, Private, October 23, 1861.

Jones, Samuel, Private, December 3, 1861.

Jones, William, Private, September 18, 1861.

Johnston, James, Private, September 24, 1861.

Joslin, Charles D., Private, September 12, 1861.

Kalbaugh, Isaac, Sergeant, October 26, 1861.

Kennedy, James, Private, October 22, 1861.

Kilroy, Thomas, Private, December 27, 1861.

King, John B., Sergeant, December 1, 1861.

Linden, James, Private, September 24, 1861.

Naughton, Michael, Private, September 12, 1861.

Pallum, James, Private, December 10, 1861.

Paris, William R., Private, October 23, 1861.

Purnell, Samuel L., Private, December 30, 1861.

Ravenscraft, James D., Private, October 16, 1861.

Schmidt, Adam, Private, October 8, 1861.

Smith, Jerome B., Private, October 28, 1861.

Tasker, Jeremiah, Private, October 24, 1861.

Wagoner, Henry C., Private, December 8, 1861.

Wagoner, Jonathan A., Private, December 8, 1861.

White, James W., Private, September 7, 1861.

Woodcock, Asbury B., Corporal, September 12, 1861.

Yupe, Adam, Private, September 12, 1861.

COMPANY E

Ackerman, Joseph, Private, November 5, 1861

Anders, George W., Private, December 11, 1861.

Bell, George W., Sergeant, November 26, 1861.

Byard, John, Private, November 26, 1861.

Chaney, Hiram, Private, December 26, 1861.

Clair, John, Private, December 11, 1861.

Crocker, James A., Private, June 18, 1861.

Dougherty, John, Corporal, December 9, 1861.

Draper, Grafton, Corporal, November 8, 1861.

Fogle, Francis, Sergeant, November 5, 1861.

Harnig, Frederick, Private, December 17, 1861.

Hays, Denton C., Corporal, November 5, 1861.

Harrison, William H., Private, December 2, 1861.

Hartsock, William H., Sergeant, November 5, 1861.

Heffner, George W., Private, December 14, 1861.

Hooker, William H., Corporal, November 12, 1861.

Iler, William, Private, December 27, 1861.

Jones, James L., Sergeant, November 11, 1861.

Keedy, Jonas, Private, November 5, 1861.

Keene, William H., Private, November 11, 1861.

Kelly, Jackson, Private, November 8, 1861.

King, Andrew J., Private, December 14, 1861.

Kolb, Martin L., Private, December 14, 1861.

Long, William H., Private, November 5, 1861.

Meazel, George L., Private, November 6, 1861.

McCallister, John, Private, November 11, 1861.

McClean, Arthur A., Private, November 25, 1861.

McLaughlin, James, Private, December 10, 1861.

Myers, William H., Private, November 12, 1861.

Nalls, George F., Private, December 12, 1861.

Need, William H., Private, November 6, 1861.

Neibergall, Cornelius, Corporal, November 21, 1861.

Ogle, William, Private, December 4, 1861.

Ohler, James, Private, December 6, 1861.

Otto, William, Private, December 28, 1861.

Ore, Franklin, Corporal, November 25, 1861.

Patterson, Joseph E., Corporal, December 9, 1861.

Penner, Grafton, Private, November 6, 1861.

Petenia, Henry, Private, December 5, 1861.

Pierpoint, John, Private, November 8, 1861.

Richmond, William H. C., Private, November 8, 1861.

Rogers, Adolphus R., Private, November 28, 1861.

Shaum, John, Private, December 3, 1861.

Sipes, Edward T., Corporal, December 3, 1861.

Stidman, John F., Sergeant, November 19, 1861.

Thoms, John, Private, November 5, 1861.

Tulley, Edward, Private, November 5, 1861.

Wagner, William T., Sergeant, December 5, 1861.

Warner, Daniel, Private, December 7, 1861.

Whitmore, George W., Private, November 19, 1861.

Winters, David, Private, December 5, 1861.

Woolridge, Richard, Private, December 5, 1861.

COMPANY F

Anders, George W., Musician, December 11, 1861.

Bitzell, Luke, Corporal, November 11, 1861.

Dimond, George, Private, December 9, 1861.

Ebberts, William, Private, November 8, 1861.

Fritzman, John, Private, November 14, 1861.

Ganoe, Charles, Private, November 14, 1861.

Golden, William, Private, December 28, 1861.

Hankle, Gotfried, Private, November 11, 1861.

Holman, Henry, Sergeant, November 14, 1861.

Jeffers, Franklin, Private, December 12, 1861.

Liess, George J., Corporal, December 3, 1861.

McAfee, John, Private, November 6, 1861.

Marsh, John H., Corporal, December 10, 1861.

Peters, Louis, Private, November 19, 1861.

Siess, George J., Private, November 19, 1861.

Sipes, Edward, Private, November 6, 1861.

Toms, John, Private, December 28, 1861.

Wagner, William, Corporal, December 11, 1861.

Wolff, George, Private, December 30, 1861.

Wolff, Samuel, Private, November 29, 1861.

COMPANY G

No one entered service in this company until January 31, 1862.

COMPANY H

Benson, Henry L., Private, September 22, 1861.
Bierbower, Jesse, Private, September 21, 1861.
Cale, Azareel, Sergeant, October 21, 1861.
Crooks, Robert C., Private, September 21, 1861.
Falkenstine, Lewis F., Musician, July 4, 1861.
Frankhouser, Martin, Private, September 5, 1861.
Haines, Daniel A., Private, September 21, 1861.
King, Albert F., Private, October 5, 1861.
King, William J., Private, October 5, 1861.
Laub, Jonathan, Private, September 21, 1861.
Mathews, Abraham, Private, September 21, 1861.
Maust, Adam, Corporal, October 14, 1861.
Metzler, Henry H., Private, December 20, 1861.
McMillen, James C., Private, September 21, 1861.
McMullen, James, Private, September 21, 1861.
Myers, John, Private, September 21, 1861.
Smith, Lucian H., Private, September 21m 1861.

COMPANY I

This company was not formed until early in 1864.

COMPANY K

This company was formed in late 1863 and early 1864.

As indicated at the beginning of this section, the source of this list is Wilmer and Jarrett's <u>History and Roster of Maryland Volunteers, War of 1860-1865.</u> The purpose of the above list is to provide the names of those who were first in "Answering the Call." What first appeared to be a relatively simple task, quickly became a laborious and time-consuming effort. The first difficulty encountered was that Wilmer and Jarrett did not alphabetize the names within each letter of the alphabet. Thus, the initial task was to unscramble the names and put them into proper order. After proceeding to compile the list in correct order, it was noticed that a number of names were being repeated in more than one company. Upon further study of the lists, it became clear that this was reflecting transfers from one company to another. Not only were names being repeated, but several were not spelled the same way the second time. For instance Milton Crutchley, who joined Company A of Cole's Cavalry and later transferred to Company I of the First Regiment of Infantry, is listed as Crutzley in the former, and correctly, as Crutchley in the latter. There are approximately a dozen other examples of this type of inconsistency which can be cited. It is not deemed necessary to specifically recite them but the reader should be cautioned against accepting the lists in Wilmer and Jarret without question. The above rosters are believed to be accurate.

There is no purpose or intent to denigrate the efforts of Messers Wilmer and Jarrett, as it is very apparent from studying their work that it required enormous time and effort to produce. They were handicapped by the necessity of deciphering the most atrocious handwriting from original muster rolls. The author can very well sympathize with them. However, one can only wonder at their failure to properly alphabetize the names. There seems to be no discernible reason or method in this, and one can only speculate that it was faulty editing or that correct order was not considered that important.

When I first conceived the idea of this book, I
envisioned a short pamphlet comprised of the letters in my
collection and a few expository remarks. An acquaintance
in the National Park Service made me aware of the
existence of the publishers. I contacted the publishing
company and received a provisional acceptance of my
manuscript on a photo-ready basis. I then proceeded to
conduct the historical research which has let to the
publication of this book. It has proved to be a very
interesting and circuitous odyssey, indeed.

I, of course, have been aware of the existence of the
Potomac Home Brigade, by virtue of my ownership of the
above-referenced documents, for many years. Upon
contacting the Historical Society of Frederick County, and
after determining that they were the repository of virtually
all of the remaining original documents relating to the scope
of this book, I was able to conclude that the letters in my
collection are unique.

I have combed all of the materials, not only in the
possession of the Historical Society in Frederick, but of
those of the Washington County Historical Society, the
Maryland State Archives in Annapolis, the Maryland
Historical Society in Baltimore, the National Archives in
Washington, DC, the Library of Congress, and the U. S.
Army Military History Institute in Carlisle, Pennsylvania. In
addition, I contacted the Allegany County Historical
Society, by letter and by phone, and determined that they

did not possess any original documents which could be included in this work.

As I initiated my search for materials to augment my own documents, I realized that the more I found, the more I needed to find. For example, the letters and many of the documents found at the Frederick County Historical Society, as well as newspaper items, refer to Major R. S. Smith, the Mustering Officer. Nowhere, in any of the original documents, was there any specific information as to who he was. I was able to find the above biographical information after an arduous search, and the splendid assistance of several of the employees, at the National Archives in Washington, DC.

Another example, is the trip I made to Petersville, Maryland to locate the grave of Francis Thomas. I knew that he was buried in the St. Mark's Churchyard and set out to see if I could find his final resting place. I found the church, and proceeded to walk through the graveyard. After about twenty-five minutes of searching each row of stones, I approached the rear of the church and chanced to see the rear of a lichen-laden marker on which was carved the inscription: "Author of the measure which gave to Maryland the Constitution of 1864 and thereby gave freedom to 90,000 human beings". Upon looking at the front of the stone, I saw the inscription "Ex-Gov Francis Thomas", and was struck with the notion, that so colorful a figure in Maryland history was buried here, and there was no historical marker to indicate the fact. I have determined to launch a lobbying effort to correct this oversight.

The above-quoted letter from John D. Ellis states that he was replying to a notice he saw in the <u>Baltimore American and Commercial Advertiser</u>. I was elated to find the exact referenced newspaper item in the microfilm records at the Maryland Historical Society Library in Baltimore.

Two of my letters were written by S. G. Prather of Clear Spring. When I discovered the newspaper notice of his death and burial at Mount Olivet Cemetery in Frederick, I decided to try to locate the grave. On a visit to the cemetery, I inquired at the office for information on the grave's location. There was no record of S. G. Prather being buried there. I later found that the soldiers who died in Frederick were temporarily interred at Mt. Olivet and subsequently removed to their respective home cemeteries.

The exact location of Camp Worman was a subject of considerable interest to me. An 1858 map of the city of Frederick indicated that Seventh Street was the last street at the city limits. Knowing that the Camp was 1.5 miles from the city limits, I clocked that distance in my car and reached the approximate area of the city water treatment plant on the Monocacy River and the Routzhan's Furniture Warehouse, which are located in a section near the beginning of Worman's Mill Road. Consultation with several fellow members of the Frederick County Historical Society has confirmed my supposition.

The mention of the Junior Hall, in the <u>Examiner</u> item on the Thanksgiving Ball, led to my locating the information on the Junior Fire Company No. 2. An article in the October 8, 1971 edition of the *Frederick Post* and a pamphlet issued on the occasion of "The 150th Anniversary of the Junior Fire Company No. 2", both provided valuable information.

I spent an afternoon searching for the grave of George W. Misner who died on January 20, 1862. He belonged to Company I, First Regiment. The facsimiles of the documents referring to his death (see above) indicate that he was from Liberty, Maryland. Names In Stone lists private Misner as being buried in Lover's Rock Cemetery located off a farm lane near Route 75. The cemetery is situated on the east side of the base of Lover's Rock on a wooded ridge about a quarter of a mile from the road. Reaching the site required a rather steep climb through bramble-choked woods. The rock is an escarpment, which on the west face, falls off to a shear fifty or sixty-foot drop. It was named for an incident when a young woman, disappointed in love, threw herself off the cliff to her death. The gravestones are mostly gone, and the ones which remain are broken, save one substantial marker. Private Misner's marker, if one existed, was not found. There is no doubt, however, that this was the site of his interment. (See the above photos.)

On the way home from my journey to Carlisle Barracks I made a stop at the Gettysburg Battlefield. At the foot of Culp's Hill a little way up the slope across the road from Spangler's Spring, is situated a very handsome monument commemorating the First Regiment of the Potomac Home Brigade Maryland Infantry. This is the spot where Colonel Maulsby and the Regiment fought on July 2nd and 3rd against fellow Marylanders serving in the Army of Northern Virginia. On one side of the monument is carved a short narration of the Regiment's exploits during the battle. The text is as follows: *JULY 2D REINFORCED THE LEFT WING BETWEEN 5 AND 6 O'CLOCK P.M. CHARGING UNDER THE IMMEDIATE DIRECTION OF GEN MEADE AND RECAPTURING THREE PIECES OF ARTILLERY. _____ JULY 3D ENGAGED THE ENEMY AT THIS POINT FROM 5 TO 6 O'CLOCK A.M. AT 11 A.M. WENT TO THE ASSISTANCE OF THE 2D DIV. 12TH CORPS, ENGAGING THE ENEMY THERE FOR ABOUT FOUR HOURS.*

On the opposite side is carved a compilation of the numbers of killed, wounded, and missing.

EFFECTIVE STRENGTH 789

CASUALTIES,
KILLED 23, WOUNDED 90,
MISSING 1, TOTAL 104

———

ORGANIZED AT FREDERICK , MD
FROM AUG. 15TH TO DEC. 13TH 1861

———

PRINCIPAL ENGAGEMENTS.
MARYLAND HEIGHTS, MD. SEPT. 13TH 1862
GETTEYSBURG, PA. JULY 2D-3D 1863.
MONOCACY, MD. JULY 9TH 1864
AND EIGHT SKIRMISHES

———

MUSTERED OUT MAY 29TH 1865.

To be able to find records of the actual people who wrote the letters and to connect them with the other materials and official documents covered by my research has been a very exhilarating and gratifying experience. The process of producing this work has been a source of many hours of enjoyment. I have had the pleasure of meeting a number of very interesting, knowledgeable, and extremely helpful people, to whom I will always be grateful.

I would venture to say that writing this book as been one of the most rewarding and interesting passages of my life. It cannot be equated with the elation I felt at the birth of my children, but ranks with whatever is in second place. Also, I must confess to feeling a certain measure of *post scriptum* depression when struck with the realization that I was finished. Another opus would thus seem to be in the offing.

ACKNOWLEDGEMENTS

The encouragement and assistance I received while conducting my research has been most gratifying. Without exception, each person who assisted me in locating a reference, answered my questions, or referred me to a useful source of information, was exceptionally professional. They have earned my eternal gratitude.

There are several individuals whom I would like to thank by name. I am thankful to Terry Adams of the National Park Service for putting me in touch with historians in the Service who cheerfully answered my questions and suggested the publisher.

Special thanks are due to Marie Washburn, Librarian, Lori Pratt, Assistant Librarian, and Velma Defibaugh, volunteer, all at the Frederick County Historical Society. Their invaluable assistance to me was crucial to my research.

I also owe a debt of gratitude to my father Dr. Norman Gary, Biology Professor Emeritus of Hood College in Frederick, Maryland. He rendered valuable assistance by arranging inter-library loans of books that were very necessary to obtain. My sister, Cynthia Smith, English teacher and grammarian of note, corrected my punctuation- a much needed service for which I am thankful.

Last, but not least, I wish to thank the many friends and family members who gave me their moral support and encouragement as I was working on the book. I thank you all.

ORIGINAL SOURCES

The Dennis Papers, original letters and documents of
        Lieutenant-Colonel Dennis, Historical Society of
        Frederick County, Inc., Frederick Maryland.

The Gary Collection, original documents owned by the
        Author.

The Maulsby Papers, original letters and documents of
        Colonel William P. Maulsby, Historical Society of
        Frederick County, Inc., Frederick, Maryland.

Potomac Home Brigade Papers, original muster rolls and
        other documents, Historical Society of Frederick
        County, Inc., Frederick, Maryland.

The Steiner Papers, original letters and documents of Major
        John Steiner, Historical Society of Frederick
        County, Inc., Frederick, Maryland.

BIBLIOGRAPHY

Andrews, Matthew Page, History of Maryland:
        Province and State, Doubleday, Doran & Company,
        Inc., Garden City, New York, 1929.

Andrews, Matthew Page, Tercentenary History of
        Maryland, S.J. Clark Publishing Company,
        Baltimore, 1925.

Basler, Roy P., Editor, The Collected Works of

Abraham Lincoln, Rutgers University Press,
New Brunswick, NJ, 1953.

Boatner III, Mark M., The Civil War Dictionary,
David McKay Company, Inc., New York,
1959.

Dyer, Frederick H., A Compendium of the War of the
Rebellion, Volume 2, Morningside, Dayton, Ohio,
1979.

Heitman, Francis B., Historical Register and
Dictionary of The United States Army,
U.S. Government Printing Office, 1903.

Holdcroft, Jacob Mehrling, Names in Stone, Ann
Arbor, Michigan, 1966.

Long, E.B., The Civil War Day by Day, Doubleday
and Company, Inc., Garden City, New York,
1971.

Lord, Francis A., They Fought For The Union, The
Stackpole Company, Harrisburg, Pennsylvania,
1960.

Lowdermilk, Will H., History of Cumberland Maryland,
Regional Publishing Company, Baltimore, 1976.
Originally published, Washington, DC, 1878.

Manakee, Harold R., Maryland in the Civil War, Maryland
Historical Society, Baltimore, 1961.

Quynn, William R., Editor, The Diary of Jacob
Engelbrecht, Historical Society of Frederick
County, Inc., Frederick, MD, 1976.

Sandburg, Carl, Abraham Lincoln The War Years,
Harcourt, Brace and Company, New York, 1939.

Scharf, J. Thomas, History of Baltimore City and County,

Regional Publishing Company, Baltimore, 1971.
Originally published, Philadelphia, 1881.

Scharf, J. Thomas, History of Western Maryland, Regional
Publishing Company, Baltimore, 1968. Originally
published, Philadelphia, 1882.

Thomas, James W. and Williams, T.J.C., History of
Allegany County Maryland, Regional Publishing
Company, Baltimore, 1969. Originally pub. 1923.

Toomey, Daniel C., The Civil War in Maryland, Toomey
Press, Baltimore, 1983.

Williams, T.J.C., History of Frederick County Maryland,
Regional Publishing Company, Baltimore, 1967.
Reprint of original edition of 1910.

Williams, Thomas J.C., A History of Washington County
Maryland, Regional Publishing Company, Baltimore,
1968.

Wilmer, L. Allison and Jarrett, J.H., History and Roster of
Maryland Volunteers, War of 1861-1865,
Guggenheimer, Weil and Company, Baltimore,
1898.

PERIODICALS CITED

The Baltimore American and Commercial Advertiser,
    Baltimore, Maryland, 1861.

The Frederick Examiner, Frederick, Maryland,
    1861.

The Maryland Union, Frederick, Maryland,
    1861.

The Post, Frederick, Maryland, October 8, 1971.

The Valley News Echo, The Potomac Edison System,
    Potomac Edison Company, Hagerstown, MD.

The Republican, Baltimore, Maryland, 1861.

Additional Periodicals Searched

The Annapolis Gazette, July-November, 1861.

The Frederick Herald, July-November, 1861.

The Hagerstown Mail, July-November 1861.

Photographic Sources

The U. S. Army Military History Institute, Photo Archives,
    Carlisle Barracks, Carlisle, PA.

The Library of Congress, Photo Duplication Section,
    Washington, DC.

Source Notes

After careful consideration of the nature of this work and the source materials, I did not deem it necessary or desirable to include traditional endnotes. As noted on the Title Page this book is based substantially on original sources. I therefore found it to be of most value to the reader to identify the provenance of the document, letter, or article in the body of the text rather than require him to thumb to the back to ascertain its origin.

Much, but not all, of the background information about the Brigade comes from the <u>History and Roster of Maryland Volunteers</u> by Wilmer and Jarrett. The names listed in Part V, The Volunteers all came from this source as well. See the above discussion of this work at the end of Part V.

When I first started collecting my own letters and documents my first source of information was Wiliams' <u>History of Frederick County Maryland</u>. Williams provides a short sketch on the Potomac Home Brigade's founding and a list of officers. For a number of years I believed this to be complete and accurate information. After commencing my formal research and having the opportunity to read original muster rolls, small but significant inaccuracies were discovered. The assistant surgeon of the First Regiment is listed as "J. Barr". The original muster roll clearly indicates that the correct name is Jacob Baer who was a prominent Frederick physician. Williams also lists the regimental surgeon as J. Boon. Dr. Boon's first name, I discovered, is Jerningham. The name is spelled out on the roll but is very difficult to read. I was able to decipher it and corroborate its accuracy by discovering his signature on several requisitions for hospital supplies. I also used this source for most of the biographical data on Francis Thomas, Colonel Maulsby, and Lieutenant-Colonel Dennis.

Williams' A History of Washington County Maryland provided me with information on Dr. A. A. Biggs (whom I thought was "Riggs" until finding his biographical sketch), Captain R. Ellsworth Cook, and J. D. Bennett. This book was also important in providing additional useful information on Francis Thomas.

Lowdermilk's History of Cumberland, Maryland was useful for information on the Second Regiment.

Thomas and Williams' History of Allegany County Maryland is the source of the letter from Colonel Thomas Johns which is quoted by permission of the publisher. This work was also useful for small tidbits of information on the Second Regiment.

Scharf's History of Western Maryland mentions several of the principals involved in the Second and Third Regiments as well as information on skirmishes and battles. Scharf served in the Confederate Army during the War and was active as a writer of local Maryland histories afterward. He had a reputation for giving a pro-Southern slant to his discussions of Civil War events and personalities.

The Valley News Echo proved to be a most excellent source of contemporary newspaper articles which I used to supplement and flesh out the other materials that I found. The article on the attempted train wreck and the failed capture of Francis Thomas provides additional insight on this most colorful character. I am indeed most appreciative of the permission to use them given by the Potomac Edison Company of Hagerstown, Maryland.

I am also grateful to the Historical Society of Frederick County, Inc. which granted permission to use the excerpts from the <u>Diary of Jacob Englebrecht</u>. These entries written by a man on the scene bearing witness to important events were especially useful to me.

The contemporary newspaper articles quoted were all located in the microfilm collection at the Maryland Historical Society Library in Baltimore.

The <u>Historical Register and Dictionary of the United States Army</u> was a major find. I had always wondered who Major R. S. Smith was and was very anxious to discover his identity if I could. After spending most of a Saturday at the National Archives in Washington, D.C., I was able to track him down.

It seemed logical that since he was Regular U. S. Army and had reached the rank of Major by July, 1861, he would have probably been in his forties and a graduate of West Point sometime between 1829 and 1834. I searched army recruiting rolls on microfilm from those years. The name of Lieutenant Smith began to appear on returns for 1835 and 1836. Incidentally, a number of recognizable names were also on these rolls. Among them were Lee and a number of others. A Lieutenant Johns was also listed and I believe him to be Thomas Johns.

Only one officer with the name of Smith was on any of these lists. Other officers with the same surname were differentiated by use of a first initial. As there were no others with the name of Smith, I concluded that this was the man I was after.

A member of the Archives staff told me that no list of commissioned U. S. officers who served in the Civil War has been compiled and said it was too bad the Major was not Confederate because such a list was compiled for that Army. She suggested that I might find him by looking at the records of applications to the Academy. These records are categorized by state and thus it was necessary to know where an individual came from in order to find his application. Many of the muster rolls show Smith enrolling recruits in and around York, Pennsylvania. Some were in Syracuse, New York as well. I made a guess that he was therefore from Pennsylvania or New York State. As we discussed my search, another staff member became interested in the quest and remarked that the Archives has an old dictionary of officers in the U. S. Army. He led me to the shelf where it is kept and handed me Heitman's book. I opened it to the S section, found the listings for Smith and ran my finger down the list to R. Smith. Only one name beginning with R has the middle initial S. The name is Richard Somers Smith from Pennsylvania, and he graduated from West Point in 1834. As I read this information, a feeling of excitement and deep satisfaction came over me. It was very apparent that I had found my man. It was gratifying to receive the congratulations of the staff members who were assisting me.

Heitman also lists the officers who served in the Potomac Home Brigade. This book was a very fortuitous find for me.

Names in Stone by Holdcroft provided the information which enabled me to locate Lovers Rock Cemetery. This abandoned graveyard is the site of George William Misner's interment.

I found Francis A. Lord's They Fought for The Union to be an amazing compilation which approaches encyclopedic dimensions. He covers all aspects of recruitment, training, equipage, weapons, organization of units, rules and regulations, supplies, and the vicissitudes of everyday life of the Union fighting man. This source provided me with the oath of allegiance administered to the volunteers and the general information about the order in which the non-commissioned officers and the commissioned officers were mustered in.

The other sources listed in the Bibliography were consulted for purposes of checking dates, names, etc.

The Potomac Home Brigade Papers in the collection of the Historical Society of Frederick County are an excellent resource which proved to be of immense usefulness. The unsigned memorandum which states the policies and procedures for recruiting and mustering volunteers I found to be particularly valuable.

The Maulsby and Dennis Papers contain many important letters and documents a number of which were integral additions to this book. A lot of very interesting material not specifically related to my topic remains and it is well worth perusing.

Of course, if I had not amassed my own collection this book, at least in its present form, would not have been possible. I have a number of other documents from the Potomac Home Brigade, but they are not germane to this book. Perhaps they will find their way into a future work.

All of the original letters and documents presented were transcribed by me, and every effort was made to ensure absolute accuracy. All errors or inaccuracies, if any, are mine alone. The reader may determine this for himself by study of the documents reproduced in facsimile. As indicated, this is the first time these documents have been published. Although I have my own opinion as to their historical significance, I will defer to others to make their own evaluation.

I did all of the photographic copying, film processing and printing the facsimiles reproduced in this book. I also took, processed the film, and printed the photographs of St. Mark's Church, the grave of Francis Thomas, Lover's Rock Cemetery, and the First Regiment Monument at Gettysburg. My daughter Kimberly took the photograph of me at the grave of William P. Maulsby.

Keith O. Gary. Photo by Kimberly E. Gary.

About the Author

Keith O. Gary was born in Washington, D.C., on October 20, 1943, and grew up in Frederick, Maryland. He received a B.A. in history from Frostburg State University, and taught high school history for several years. Later he received his M.Ed. degree in remedial reading from the University of Maryland at College Park.

In 1983 Mr. Gary began a career in the field of cameras and photography. He now works for a professional photographic laboratory as their Customer Service Manager and black and white photo technician. He also works as a professional free-lance photographer. Mr. Gary is divorced, has two grown children, a son and a daughter, and currently lives in historic Greenbelt, Maryland.